MW00605884

TALIBAN
SAFARI

TALIBAN
SAFARI

ONE DAY IN THE
SURKHAGAN VALLEY

Paul Darling

University Press of Kansas

All photographs belong to the author.

Published by the University Press of Kansas (Lawrence, Kansas 66045),
which was organized by the Kansas Board of Regents and is operated
and funded by Emporia State University, Fort Hays State University,
Kansas State University, Pittsburg State University, the University
of Kansas, and Wichita State University.

Library of Congress Cataloging-in-Publication Data
Names: Darling, Paul (Paul Thomas), author.
Title: Taliban safari : one day in the Surkhagan Valley / Paul Darling.
Description: Lawrence, Kansas : University Press of Kansas, [2019]
Identifiers: LCCN 2018058241
ISBN 9780700627844 (cloth : alk. paper)
ISBN 9780700627851 (ebook)
Subjects: LCSH: Darling, Paul (Paul Thomas) | Afghan War, 2001– —
Personal narratives, American. | Taliban. | Afghan War, 2001– —
Campaigns—Afghanistan—Zabul. | United States. Army—Officers—
Biography. | Alaska. Army National Guard—Biography. | Soldiers—United
States—Biography. | United States. Army—Military life—History—21st
century. | Afghan War, 2001– —United States.
Classification: LCC DS371.413 .D37 2019 | DDC 958.104/742—dc23
LC record available at https://lccn.loc.gov/2018058241.

British Library Cataloguing-in-Publication Data is available.

Printed in the United States of America

10 9 8 7 6 5 4 3 2 1

FOR GRETCHEN

CONTENTS

ABBREVIATIONS AND ACRONYMS

ACU	Army combat uniform
ANA	Afghan National Army
ANP	Afghan National Police
ANSF	Afghan National Security Forces
BFT	Blue force tracker. Computer used to track the battlefield and communicate outside radio range.
COP	Combat outpost. A small permanent base of eight to fifty soldiers.
ETT	Embedded transition team. Americans dedicated to mentoring the Afghan National Army.
FOB	Forward operating base. A fairly large camp of at least fifty soldiers.
HMMWV	High-mobility, multipurpose wheeled vehicle. The Jeep of the twenty-first century.
ICOM radio	Commercial radio used by the Taliban for tactical communications.
IED	Improvised explosive device. Specifically, a homemade explosive device but used colloquially to describe any explosive weapon not fired from a cannon or likewise.
IGoA	Islamic Government of Afghanistan
Inshallah	Arabic: "If Allah wills it."
ISAF	International Security Assistance Force
ISR	Intelligence, surveillance, and reconnaissance
klicks	kilometers
MBITR	Multiband inter/intra team radio
Medevac	Medical evacuation. Can be used to describe a ground or air evacuation, but often used as a shorthand term to describe aerial units dedicated to medical transport of wounded soldiers.

NCO   non–commissioned officer
NDS   National Directorate of Security
net   network
PHQ   Police headquarters
PID   Positive identification
PMT   Police mentor team. Americans dedicated to mentoring
             the Afghan National Police.
PZ   Pickup zone
RPG   RPG is a transliteration of a Russian abbreviation
             (*ruchnoy protivotankoviy granatomyot*), which translates to
             the English phrase "handheld antitank grenade launcher."
             Thus *rocket-propelled grenade* is a backronym.
SA   Situational awareness. Understanding of the current
             environment.
SAPI   small arms protective insert
SATCOM   Satellite communications
SF   Special Forces. US Army Special Operations Unit formed
             in the 1950s dedicated to training foreign forces.
SITREP   Situation report
SOP   Standard operating procedure
TC   Tank commander. Used to describe the senior occupant
             of any military ground vehicle.
terp   interpreter
TIC   Troops in contact
TOC   tactical operations center
UAH   Up-armored HMMWV
UAVs   Unmanned aerial vehicles. Commonly called drones.
VBIED   Vehicle-borne improvised explosive device
VIC   Vehicle

ACKNOWLEDGMENTS

Dedicating a book to your wife is cliché, but this book was truly written for her to read. To explain "what it was like." To try, somehow, to justify my voluntary yearlong absence.

The format and subtitle are stolen shamelessly from Alexander Solzhenitsyn's classic novel *One Day in the Life of Ivan Denisovich*. But this is no novel. It is as honest and accurate as memory could make it. I deliberately completed the first draft within a year of the actual events to maintain an honest narrative of what actually happened, as opposed to what I wish had happened or wished I had done. On the advice of a friend who is a lawyer and an outstanding officer, only one small detail was changed. Those with experience in close combat will probably recognize it. All others will neither notice nor care.

Although the book was not written for the combat veteran, I hope veterans will appreciate it. Extraneous details of the mundane reality of deployed life permeate; they were as much an influence as the actual combat. If the story seems monotonous at times, it reflects reality. Even on an extraordinary day, there are only so many ways to describe nearly ten hours in an armored car, sweating. The book originally contained what I considered witty and astute observations of the greater mission in Afghanistan. My editor and the reviewers she sent the manuscript to thought otherwise, and the majority of those observations have been excised, no doubt to the relief of readers.

For the military professional, the best prologue will be found in my article in *Military Review* (July–August 2011), "The Five Fights of the Surkhagan and the Future of ISAF."

While I consider all the men I served with that year heroes, this is not a book about heroism. It is merely the memory of one man and one day in Afghanistan.

My deepest thanks go out to Les Grau, without whose efforts this book would never have been published and whose writing helped me, and countless others, return home safe from Afghanistan, and to Lieutenant Commander Justin Lawlor, whose encouragement got me writing and whose criticism made it readable. Finally, to my wife, Gretchen: for everything.

Battles, Ambushes Kill around 30 in Afghanistan
Associated Press, June 7, 2009

KABUL: A joint Afghan and US-led coalition operation against insurgents in southern Afghanistan killed more than 20 Taliban fighters today, while a militant ambush in the northwest killed four policemen, officials said.

The joint operation in Zabul province included ground forces and airstrikes. The battle killed more than 20 Taliban, said provincial police chief Abdul Rahman Sarjung [*sic*]. After the operation, a roadside bomb exploded and killed one Afghan policeman as the forces was [*sic*] returning to base, he said.

TALIBAN
SAFARI

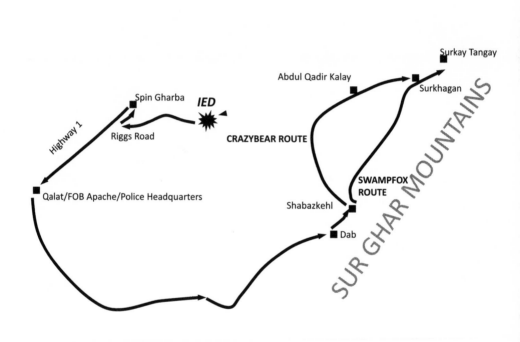

1

START POINT

0345.

My watch starts beeping and I shift to shut it off. M.Sgt. Rob Apel, my noncommissioned officer in charge who shares my hooch, isn't going today. No real reason not to go; no real reason to go, either. I hope I didn't wake him up, but he snores next to my bunk.

Five days ago, he was in a good fight. Not as good as everyone thinks, but still good. Three dead Taliban for sure, one a commander. An improvised explosive device planter. Two months ago, one of his bombs killed a Romanian captain whose job was to search for IEDs (improvised explosive devices). Well, that Romanian captain found one and it was planted by a Taliban. I was there minutes after it happened. I watched his soldiers, some teary eyed, following with their eyes the medevac helicopter carrying his lifeless body away on the long and final journey home. Now the Taliban responsible for that death is dead, but no one knows exactly who killed him. I was there right after the fight (I have an unenviable ability to *just* miss a firefight) as we swept the hills for weapons, equipment, and enemy killed in action. Especially bodies. I was the one that actually found his body. The night vision goggles helped a lot. But I was proud I saw it before the Afghan police did, regardless. I almost never see things before the Afghans. They see everything before I do. I have ten-power binoculars and a four-power scope on my rifle and I still don't see what they see. Amazing. Especially when I have been told they were all blind. But I found that body, and the back of his head was blown open.

The front didn't look too bad; the guy took something in the left eye and that was gone or at least destroyed to the point of being unrecognizable. But the rest of his face looked OK. He was wearing a brownish-green field jacket. The Taliban put those on before battle. Osama bin Laden wore a field jacket in all his pictures and videos, as prominent as his captured, miniaturized AK-47. Now all the Taliban commanders wear them when they aren't trying to hide among the civilians. So this guy missing the back of his head was legit. Sometimes I wonder after the fight, but not this time. Big beard, an ICOM radio (the Taliban's second-most preferred communication device after the cell phone). His weapon was gone; someone who didn't die reacted quickly enough to grab it in his effective retreat. The stories from the troops say he was shot by a 40mm round that didn't explode. If you aren't far enough away, the round won't arm and won't explode. But an eye socket is smaller than forty millimeters, so if he had been shot by a 40mm round, more of the front would be missing. Rob thinks he shot him with his rifle. He might have. He probably did. But nobody knows for sure. Nobody ever has the same view of things during or after a battle. The fact is Rob shot *at* him, and that's really what matters. Not everybody shoots when the bad guys are around. But Rob isn't going to be shooting anybody today. Not unless things go really wrong.

0345. I am able to turn the watch off so quickly because I am already awake. I didn't get to sleep until 2300 the night before, yet I still wake up fifteen minutes before my alarm. I lie in bed, eyes wide open, going through today's planned events and earlier failures. Anticipating what I am going to do, what the enemy is going to do, what I am going to do about the enemy; endless iterations of IF:THEN.

I'm tired, but not as tired as I should be. This is my mission—a first for the province, as far as I know. Helicopters and UAVs (unmanned aerial vehicles) along with a dedicated ground force moving to the bad guys, wherever they may be, rather than to a predetermined location. We call the UAVs "ISR"—intelligence, surveillance, and reconnaissance. That's what they do. More to the point, that's what I need and I finally got it. The operation is happening in a place called the Surkhagan Valley. It is in the district of Qalat, which is in the province of Zabul. That's in southern Afghanistan and that's where my soldiers and I fight alongside of (ideally) and in front of (too often) the Afghan National Police (ANP). If Afghanistan is the ass crack of the world (Asscrackistan), then Zabul is its unwashed anus.

0345. Within a minute I swing around and start to get dressed in the dark. Rob is awake but he can go back to sleep if I stay quiet enough. The pants are actually designed for pilots—lots of zippers and fireproof. The zippers are good. The pants they issue the nonpilots have crap Velcro and everything falls out of the pockets. Plus, there aren't enough pockets. In my many pockets, I have some mocha-flavored gels to snack on.

Originally designed for runners, the gels taste pretty good and don't take up much room—handy while walking in all my gear. A small tube of sunscreen is also in one of the pockets; a tan note pad that doesn't disintegrate in the rain is in another. Not that it rains during this time of year, but still. That's on my left side. My right pocket has a combat tourniquet. As I was taught at Camp Funston, if I can stop the bleeding, the guy is generally going to live. But that tourniquet isn't really there for the other guy, it is for me. If I lose a limb, I can apply the tourniquet by myself. It is designed to be used with one hand.

The boots are nice and light. I bought them when I first came over to Afghanistan because my other boots were too hot. That was when the highs were in the 80s. Now they are in the 100s. The tread is falling apart, not from missions but from walking around the FOB (forward operating base). There is gravel everywhere on the FOB and it tears up my soles. And I spend too much of my time on the FOB.

Everybody hates the FOB, or at least they say they do. The FOB is safe and boring. It is my home while I am in Afghanistan. A FOB is a bigger combat outpost (COP). Nicer. Comfier. Ours is co-located with the Afghan National Army (ANA) brigade headquarters. Over 1,000 Afghan soldiers plus 100 Americans.

My wonderful boots on, I find my combat shirt in the dark. The fabric is so unique that I find it by touch. The combat shirt highlights the ironic stupidity that is the army at times. The army standard uniform stateside is called the ACU (army combat uniform). But I can't wear it in combat. No. The ACU is not fire retardant. Instead, when I deployed, I was issued the FRACU. Pronounced *frak-you*. Flame-retardant ACU. But even that is replaced with the army combat shirt. The army issues body armor that can stop almost any bullet. I always wear it when outside the wire. But if it can stop a bullet, it can also stop a cooling breeze or stop perspiration from evaporating. It is hot to wear. So some smart guy took a t-shirt and sewed FRACU sleeves to it. It looked professional, was cooling and comfortable, reduced the risk of heat exhaustion, and didn't cost more. The FOB sergeant major community nearly had a collective stroke. But amazingly, rather than ban them, they decided to make a commercial version of the army combat shirt. It was minimalist: two zippered pockets on the sleeves; a place for my unit patch on the left; name, rank, and American flag on my right. All attached by the ubiquitous Velcro (hook and pile tape in the army vernacular). A very light fabric on the torso flanked by reinforced sleeves with elbow pads built in. The elbow pads even have nubs, so when I'm firing my rifle or machine gun my elbows won't slip on concrete. Sometimes the army gets things right. But most FOBs don't let you wear them, even if you're just stopping at the base temporarily while on a mission.

It has only been two minutes since my alarm went off, and I don't have to meet up at the trucks until 0400. Coffee time. The coffee has been sitting since yesterday, but that doesn't matter. While I may not be particularly tired after a whole four hours of sleep, that doesn't mean I don't want coffee. I grab my hat and step out into the wonderfully cool morning. As I shut the door, I hear squeaking from Rob's bed as he rolls over. He'll get back to sleep just in time to wake up again when I return to grab the rest of my gear.

Entering the chow hall, I realize I am not the first one up. Someone else from the team is there. We nod to each other, both lost in our own thoughts. Nobody talks much at 0400, certainly not before a long mission. I grab my cup of coffee and head to the snacks sitting on the makeshift table. Cheap beef jerky and pop tarts. That should work. The fruit assortment is lacking and what remains looks inedible. I can sometimes arrange for the cooks to get up early and make breakfast when I have an early day, but not this early. That would be rude. And the cooks, civilians all, I like.

Snacks in hand, I move to our HMMWVs (pronounced *humvees*) parked ten meters away from my hooch. The whole FOB is maybe 150 meters by 150 meters. I drop the snacks into my goodie box hiding behind my computer by my seat and sip the coffee, which is as bad as I feared. Three or four sips later I throw it down and toss the Styrofoam cup into the trash. It is time to get my stuff and my truck ready.

Back at the hooch, I try to be quiet and let Rob sleep but find I can't. I grab my helmet, rifle, and body armor. My "go bag" is already in the trunk of the HMMWV. The go bag has the stuff I might need: night vision goggles (NVGs), extra ammo, some star clusters (flares). I also have a laser pointer that can only be seen by NVGs. I was supposed to use it to mark targets for aircraft or other friendlies. I used to keep it on my vest, but after a while it got demoted to the go bag. I have a signaling mirror, another archaic throwback. It is designed to signal aircraft. As if they couldn't see my vehicles. More beef jerky and mocha packets. Aside from the ammo and food, nothing in the bag has been used in the past seven months.

Rob wishes me an exhaustion-muffled and halfhearted, "Good luck." I walk to my HMMWV and drop my helmet and weapon onto my seat, my vest onto the hood.

Sergeant Dhakal joins me at the HMMWV. He is going to be my gunner today. A Nepalese, he is aggressive and speaks with a nearly unintelligible accent over the radio. He is also an Illinois guardsman, along with the rest of my team, except my medic, who is a newly promoted navy corpsman not old enough to drink. Dhakal, who has picked up the less-than-prized nickname Dookie, has one of the famous Gurkha knives. This knife, like so many other famous artifacts, is much less impressive up close. For today, however, his tools are a bit more modern and impersonal. A .50-caliber machine gun mounted in the HMMWV's turret is his primary weapon system. Robust and powerful, it can also be finicky as well as a bit of overkill. So bolted against the righthand side of the turret is a secondary weapon system, the M240 machine gun. Known as the GPMG (general-purpose machine gun) or MAG-58, this gun is the standard for medium machine guns and will work, as long as it is lubricated, all day long. In the turret, the machine guns have several hundred rounds of ammunition immediately ready, as well as more than 2,000 additional rounds inside the HMMWV. Dhakal also has his M4 carbine, the shortened and more popular cousin of the M16. Finally, the despised but dependable M9 Beretta pistol hangs from his hip in a ten-dollar Afghan-made holster.

My driver, a specialist named Moore, is the more common soldier variety. Another Illinois guardsman, he is from a small town, like most of his compatriots. Both Moore and Dhakal were new replacements transferred from eastern Afghanistan. That is why they are on my crew. At this point, everyone prefers to work with people they know.

Staff sergeant Genovese is a twenty-four-year-old traditional (part-time) guardsman who has basically been in uniform full time for the past two years. Also known as a "guard bum," Genovese is on his second deployment. The first was to Iraq. He had since been to both Ranger and Airborne schools, which is uncommon in the guard for anyone. To Genovese, soldiering was a video game, one he liked to turn off when it was no longer interesting. Single and restless, he sought adventure, and Zabul provided more than enough. His aggressive attitude makes him a natural leader in the team and he gets people to follow him, if at times begrudgingly. His stated mission in Afghanistan is: 1. Kill Taliban and 2. Get jacked (in shape) and tanned.

In this quest for physical self-congratulatory improvement mixed with Taliban hunting, Genovese is accompanied by newly promoted staff sergeant Gregory, also age twenty-four. Gregory is as pale as Genovese is naturally tan, but they both work out two to three times a day, even after missions. Gregory is married and has a young son. He is more deliberate and contemplative than Genovese, but also more aggressive in a fight. For natural abilities as a soldier, Gregory would be hard to match. He is more disciplined than Genovese and understands the importance of the more mundane tasks involved in soldiering and steps up to get them done, even though he doesn't enjoy them. In the absence of Genovese, I could probably trust Gregory to run a mission on his own. But that wasn't the case, so it wasn't an option. Both command their own vehicles with assorted Afghan police in tow. I also imagine fifty years hence they will be calling each other on their birthdays.

A standard crew for the HMMWV is three: driver, gunner, and tank/track commander (TC). A throwback to a more traditional age, this designation refers to the ranking person in the vehicle. Responsible for everything the crew does, this person is supposed to maintain overall SA (situational awareness): ensuring the gunners are engaging the right targets and the driver is going the right way. Prior to the mission, each person has certain individual jobs to perform getting the HMMWV ready. The driver will pop the hood to check fluids and ensure the belts aren't cracked. A once-over. For short missions or admin moves, this cursory check may take twenty seconds. Today the drivers are spending a few extra minutes. It is going to be at least a twelve-hour mission, and there are few things worse than being towed home. The TC's job is to get the communications systems running. There are two standard radios, both MBITRs (multiband inter/intra team radios). The MBITR uses a single rechargeable battery that lasts for about twelve hours and the mount in the vehicle recharges the battery, which can be swapped with any other battery. It operates on several bands and can also be used for satellite communication, assuming it has the proper antenna. In addition to the two in my vehicle, I have one on my back, covered slightly by my CamelBak canteen. While the MBITR can do satellite communications (SATCOM), I have a dedicated satellite communications device mounted on top of the two MBITR mounts. Capable of worldwide communications, it is one of the devices I can use to call for help. And finally, the BFT (blue force tracker)—a satellite-linked, GPS-accurate computer marvel that allows me to email anybody in Afghanistan from anywhere in Afghanistan. It shows me exactly where everybody else is and has every map required, including satellite imagery. As with so many other technical achievements, most people can only use a fraction of its capabilities. Operations like today's, which would be foolhardy in the absence of this technology, become commonplace. If anything can burn off Clausewitz's "fog of war," it's the BFT. It looks like a heavily armored personal computer and is always in view of the TC. It will be the primary means of communication with the "battle space owner," otherwise known as the guy who can help me if things go bad. Those ISR and helicopters I asked for are only good if I can talk to them. I turn on all my comms (communications) and send a quick message to Task Force Zabul, the battle space owner. The touch screen doubles as my keyboard and is awkward to use. Messages are invariably short: "ISR on station?" "RGR. TB at OBJ." Roger. Taliban at objective. Yes, the ISR is overhead. Yes, we have found the enemy.

My checks complete, it's time for the mission briefing. I look around to see if everyone has finished checking their vehicles. The group huddles into an aboveground bomb shelter. A few people smoke. A few drink some water, their heads down in thought. No one is talking. Since it is so early in the morning, the jokes are kept to a minimum. "Alright, you guys all remember the plan," I begin. Most shake their heads. I realize I had only briefed a few people the night before. I assumed that they would spread the word. And I had assumed wrong. Another one of those mundane soldier tasks that Geno had dispensed with. Spreading out the map, I brief the plan again. It's a simple plan. I, with Team Swampfox, will move with ANP south to Suri, a part of Shinkay district. Move toward the Dab Pass and conduct a dismounted presence patrol in the village of Shabazkehl. This is fancy talk for walking around in a village talking with people. Move out of Shabazkehl and as quickly as possible toward the enemy while the Apache helicopters either kill them or keep them from escaping.

First, I am going to move south so the enemy won't immediately flee. It would take us at least three hours to get to Surkhagan. The enemy needs only thirty minutes to escape to the mountains and out of sight. It should take less than an hour to get from Shabazkehl to Surkhagan. The newly arrived Apache helicopters will do the killing today; we are merely driving the game. Getting the enemy to move into the open, away from the villages. Away from the civilians and out in the open, where the chain guns and rockets of the helicopters could slaughter them. No more aimless Taliban safaris; I intend to harvest the enemy. Until now, they always had the advantage of mobility. But Taliban motorcycles don't move faster than helicopters. Today I have all the advantages. At least that is the theory. Another of my teams, Nomad, will move from the north. They have another mission first, which will throw off the enemy as to their true objectives. They will leave a little later in the day. Most days I expect to meet the enemy, but I could rarely plan for a big fight. Today should be different.

I tell my team the ISR has found Taliban where we are going. Smiles break out, but not nervous smiles. Driving around for hours chasing ghosts is exhausting. The IEDs are everywhere, as I was reminded less than a month ago in the exact same place where I was going today. At least I know our efforts won't be wasted. The soldiers appreciate that. A final request for questions meets silence. It is quiet and somewhat awkward. All eyes are on me as they patiently await the final word. At a loss for something more profound to say, I mutter a simple, "Mount up, commo checks, and let's get out of here," and close the briefing.

I make my way to my truck and throw on my body armor and helmet. The body armor has the absolute necessities for combat. Up front is my pistol, attached in cross-draw fashion high on my chest. The only ammunition is what is in the magazine well. If I need more than fifteen rounds of 9mm, I am doing something wrong. Directly below, on the flap, are six thirty-round magazines for my rifle. Two of the magazines are all tracer ammunition, meaning that the bullets burn a trail showing their flight. But the trails aren't for me to see. I use them to show others where to shoot. To the right of the magazines is a pouch for a red smoke grenade. Smoke is essential. It can hide me from my enemies and it can show my position for friendlies. It is also used to mark landing locations for helicopters. Next to that is another pouch for my GPS and binoculars. Both are quite small and both amazingly useful when I need them. Then, on my far right, is my IFAK (individual first aid kit). Crammed in this one small pouch are all the essential medical supplies. Tape, gauze, another tourniquet, and combat gauze with a chemical that will stop any bleeding. An izzy (Israeli) pressure dressing. Scissors. A tube that goes through the nostril to aid breathing. Finally, an EpiPen (epinephrine auto-injector), just in case of a bee sting, which I happen to be allergic to. To the left of my magazines are two hand grenades and a flash bang (which won't hurt but will distract an enemy—to be used if there may be civilians mixed with enemies).

On my vest rests a compass in a thirdhand grenade pouch. I swore coming out that I would never need or carry hand grenades. Within a month in Zabul, I found myself swearing never to leave them behind again. Afghanistan's very common mud walls are all but impervious to bullets, but they can't stop a hand grenade from coming over the top of them. Grenades are heavy and dangerous to everyone around. But sometimes they are the only thing that will work, so I carry two. On my left shoulder strap is a parachute cord-cutter used to cut seat belts quickly; being burned alive while trapped in a seat belt was a shared nightmare for everyone. My right shoulder is clear. Previously a strobe light was there, but there's a smaller strobe/flashlight mounted on my helmet, along with an NVG mount. On the back of the vest are mounted my MBITR and a CamelBak water carrier. Water is essential when moving in the hills. The antenna for the MBITR snakes through the dozens of straps on the back of my armor. The range of the radio is highly dependent upon terrain. But in less than a minute I can have a six-foot antenna that can reach and receive for miles. Inside the vest are my SAPI (small arms protective insert) plates, which can stop any bullet fired by the enemy. Heavy and stiff, SAPIs are not comfortable, but highly comforting. This martial ensemble, with helmet, comes to about fifty pounds. This is my minimum fighting load. My enemy carries less than half that amount.

I don my gear by throwing it over my head and securing it with the large Velcro patches. This move is replicated by all the soldiers on the team at roughly the same time. The gunners climb to the top of the HMMWVs and lower themselves down. Drivers get behind the wheel and move the ignition switch a single click, allowing the diesel engines' glow plugs to pre-warm the cylinders. Within seconds, the HMMWVs easily start. The radios are already on, and everyone puts on their Bose headsets. All keep one headphone flipped up on the helmet away from the ear to listen for ambient noise. Commo checks ring out and conclude quickly. Unbidden, the lead vehicle moves toward the front gate. The previous evening, I coordinated with the navy-staffed FOB detachment to make sure the gate was open at 0500. Usually it is locked until 0700. A female sailor is there, smiling and waving. Neither action appears too forced in spite of the early hour. A sharp left, and we are through the gate and out of the FOB.

2

LINE OF DEPARTURE

0501.

I'm outside the gate of the FOB, but I'm not in "Indian country" yet. FOB Apache is nestled on the back side of the Afghan National Army's 2nd Brigade, 205th Corps headquarters. In the US Army, we have the same nomenclature, but with a twist. There is usually a division between a brigade and a corps: three to four brigades in a division, two to four divisions in a corps. The Afghans skipped division. Might be a math issue. Also, whereas we have battalions in a brigade, the Afghans have *kandaks*. The brigade in Zabul Province has five kandaks: three infantry, one combat support (consisting of engineer-type units), and one combat service support (logistics, etc.). However, the concept of how combat support and combat service support works is somewhat lost. So the combat support unit acts as a regular infantry kandak and the combat service support kandak does the same around Qalat City.

I also have to deal with the myth of the Afghan warrior. The vast majority of Afghans I fight with aren't warriors. They are bandits. They fight when success is ensured and profit potential exists. Fighting Taliban changes nothing. The police and army get paid whether or not they fight Taliban. However, I have means at my disposal to "encourage" them to fight. Humiliation is one, but I can quickly wear that out. Good report cards are another. Money received from Kabul can be influenced by American reports sent up once a month. Access to supplies is another. How hard the mentor pushes for supplies can influence how quickly it comes from Kabul. The mentors for the ANA aren't graded on results, they are graded on the same things the US Army is graded on when it isn't fighting: training status, personnel numbers, and equipment readiness. So as long as those things look good, the mentors look good, the Afghans look good. Everybody wins, including the Taliban. Especially the Taliban. Fighting can really put a ding in your readiness numbers. As the Russian Grand Duke Constantine is often quoted as saying, "I detest war; it spoils an army." For the ANA, it might not be so complex. A man can get killed out there. For a Tajik, killing a Pashtun is fine; dying for one isn't.

At 0500, however, these thoughts are secondary to the rhythm of accelerate-and-brake as we make our way out of the ANA base. Afghans, like those of many other nonwestern cultures, don't *do* traffic laws. Especially speed limits. Positively an affront to one's masculinity, or so it would appear. So the easy solution is to place speed bumps every hundred meters to keep the speed down. It works, to a degree. With military vehicles (and military fuel) it becomes a contest to see how fast one can drive before slamming on the brakes. The up-armored HMMWVs (UAHs) have powerful engines, but are still not the quickest off the line, dragging eight tons of steel along with them. So the movement is more like that of an inchworm. The conversation remains minimal, not the least because I can't understand half of what Dhakal says over the radio and Moore knows better than to talk too much this early in the morning. I continue to go over the rough plan in my head and try to determine exactly what to tell the province's deputy chief of police, Julani, when I see him. I figure I can tell him everything at this point, as he probably already knows what I am planning to do. Julani is a tough nut to crack. My first week in Zabul, I was told that he is definitely in the employ of the Taliban. Two weeks later, he drove me straight toward the Taliban, where we killed the second-highest-ranking Taliban in the province. The biggest HVT (high-value target) ever killed in Zabul. All because of Julani. Hardly sounds like a bad guy, but I can't be sure. I can never be sure.

Close to the end of the base, I pass the "terp camp." Technically, my terps (interpreters) live here. And the technicality rests on two issues. My team, Crazybear, has three terps: Aziz, Ramazan, and Highlander. Aziz doesn't speak Pashto and Ramazan doesn't speak English. This makes those two worthless right off the bat. And Highlander is a pussy. Which, while not worthless entirely, makes him worthless for today's mission. I use him for day-to-day stuff. His language skills are very good. However, I get the feeling that the police don't trust him. Whether it's because he might be Taliban or whether it's because he's so clearly a pussy, I don't know. But for important stuff, I can't use any of the terps assigned to me. So, since my three terps aren't coming today, I am stealing Swampfox's terps for this fight. They live in FOB Apache with Swampfox's civilian trainers. This drives the embedded transition teams (ETTs) crazy. They claim, accurately, that it violates the KBR (Kellog, Brown, and Root) contract. However, the space they take up wouldn't be used, anyway. They eat in the American chow hall, but all interpreters are allowed to do this. The real reason it drives them crazy is because it reinforces the fact that the PMTs (police mentor teams) are out fighting and the ETTs aren't. PMTs roll within minutes of notification of possible Taliban. The ETTs take hours, if they roll at all. Having terps living with the mentors decreases the response time, increases the terps' English skills, and builds trust. The only good reason not to have terps live with us is that you don't trust them or you don't want them around. In the PMT world, those aren't good reasons. The civilians they live with would ordinarily be coming with us today, but not right now. Their company's contract is up for renewal and they have to appear to be doing everything and nothing at the same time.

A few months back, they were with Swampfox during a TIC (troops in contact) and fired some rounds at the Taliban. This was before I got to Zabul. They dutifully reported what happened and now they are banned from going out anywhere except police headquarters (PHQ), which really sucks for them and for us. There simply aren't too many people I trust out there, and that pulled three more US guys who knew what they were doing. Plus, we are supposed to be a team in developing the Afghans. The police have more respect for those who go on combat missions, which my civilian guys don't do anymore. Not for lack of desire or experience. It doesn't make them worthless; far from it. They are still critical in helping with the logistics and paperwork of keeping the fledgling ANP up and running. When we inspected the jail in Qalat, we took a guy who had worked in a city jail in Southern California with us and he was a critical help in figuring out how to enroll the prisoners there into our biometrics program.

I have handheld biometrics computers. They can take fingerprints, scan irises, and put the names of the people I was enrolling into a vast computer database, otherwise known as "HIIDEing" them into the system, after the name of the equipment, the handheld interagency identity detection equipment (HIIDE). There were about seventy prisoners there at the Qalat City jail. It probably should have held about thirty. Another vestige of the days when Afghanistan was controlled by Russia, the jail looked like a miniature castle on a hill. As I walked up to it, the sewage flowed down in an open dirt ditch next to the road. The structure was several stories high, but no more than 500 square meters at the base. The cells were used as offices and one large area was used to house the prisoners. The civilian mentor knew how to segregate prisoners. He ensured that the guys working with the prisoners weren't armed but had someone nearby who was—all those things that soldiers don't know but cops do. I probably couldn't do any of the combat missions without the civilians keeping the lights running. And they want to get out, but first they have to keep the contracts running. And that means keeping a low profile. And killing Taliban might get someone noticed. At least they got to sleep in.

We pass the terp camp, where my terps who aren't coming are sleeping. The camp is its own little walled castle—whether to keep the ANA out or the terps in is unclear. What goes on inside those walls I don't like to think about. They call it man-love Thursday, but it isn't limited to Thursdays. Afghan society so isolates women that the men do what men do in prison. It is not as obvious as I had been told by others, most of whom never really dealt with Afghans, anyway. But it does happen. And then we pass by the ever-present volleyball court, adjacent to the terp camp. Afghans love to play volleyball but they're horrible at it. They have fun, and that's what matters, I guess. I played them once and was kind of surprised at how bad they were, considering how much they play. As I approach the gate to the Afghan army camp, we drive through the weaving chicane created by the omnipresent Hesco bastions, and the radios come to life again. "VIC 1, weapons hot, jam on." Vehicle number one in the convoy, weapons are loaded and the electronic countermeasures designed to stop remote-controlled IEDs from exploding is on and operating properly. VIC 2 and VIC 3 echo. It took a month just to get the basic radio procedures working when I arrived. Sometimes they still don't report properly. On admin runs to the PHQ or FOB Lagman on the other side of Qalat City, the standards almost invariably slip. They shouldn't, and I constantly remind them. But that's the problem with young, inexperienced soldiers. The video game can get boring. Today's mission is different, so the tone is different—more focused, less joking. Or maybe it's the early morning hour. I hope it is the former but sheepishly admit to myself it is almost certainly the latter.

As we descend the hill, to my left is what is known as Alexander's castle, a huge one hundred-square-meter mud castle on top of the largest hill dominating Qalat City. Legend has it that Alexander the Great built it when he came to Afghanistan, leaving behind a detachment of Macedonian soldiers. Highway 1 is supposedly the route Alexander took on his way to India. While the archeological evidence may not all be there, the basic fundamental military principle of "seize the high ground" applies as much now as it did during Alexander's time. Not coincidentally, the Afghan army base is on the next-highest hill. The castle is about 300 meters away from the access road we are traveling down to Qalat City. Between the road and the castle are the mud huts of dozens of families. Usually—but not this early—the kids crowd around the vehicles, hoping for us to toss out candy. They will sprint alongside my vehicle, occasionally tripping into the open ditch that serves as the Qalat sewage system. We laugh every time because it is visually funny. But at the same time, we all feel for these kids. They have the same bright, curious eyes as our own children. The girls are not old enough to be enveloped in their own personal tents known as the *burqa,* or burka. But I know that their fate awaits. Married at ten, consummated at twelve, pregnant by fourteen, dead by forty. Can we save them through this Taliban safari we are taking? Can we change a society unaltered in two thousand years? Overcome the negative aspects of traditional Pashtonwalli and Islam? Five years? Ten? A generation? These are the key questions that I can never answer but often ask. Just not today.

It is not yet dawn, but I can see fine without the lights. There are street lights in Qalat along the main road, but they have been turned off. The only generator in town is intermittent at best due to fuel costs. Americans (or international donors) bought the generators, but the fuel is on the Afghan government. And Qalat doesn't get a lot of fuel. The governor constantly asks for more fuel, to which the local US State Department representative can only say, "Ask your government." They play this game a lot. The State Department rep is new, a former marine engineer officer who served in Iraq. This is his first state department gig. He seems capable, but I am only just getting to know him. His predecessor was a female public affairs type. They are the senior civilian representatives for a key province in Afghanistan: a public affairs person and someone in his very first job. I wonder how serious we as a nation are about this governance thing when they send unqualified folks with no assets to advise a provincial government. I also wonder how many State Department people they have back in Kabul. Task Force Zabul keeps a list of funny things heard around the campfire. One of them was from Elizabeth, the former State Department rep. She said, "When I go to Kabul and tell people I work in Zabul, they laugh at me." The joke's on us. Kabul, with its swarming masses of the cocktail party set, isn't where we are going to win this war. It is in places like Zabul, where the lone person trying to teach governance is a public affairs specialist who gets laughed at. Hilarious.

We continue down the access road with Alexander's castle to my left and a wrecked area of ad hoc tents and shanties on my right. This used to be a main market, but the previous governor had it torn down. The common rumor is that he was bribed to help competing markets in a different area. Everybody knows, but there really isn't anything they can do about it. Governors are appointed by Afghanistan's president, Hamid Karzai, not elected by the people. No accountability and nothing the locals can do about it. *Why lose sleep when I have already lost my home and livelihood?* One of our many talking points is that we are bringing "Western-style democracy." I'll have to pardon the Afghans for being less than enthused. Not that a Taliban governor would have been any different, but at least they wear the guise of Islam to justify their position. Now they can blame the Americans, and the Taliban can hold the sacred Koran as their instruction manual. In the local Afghans' eyes there is no justification for the provincial governors except the whims of the "American puppet, Karzai." War is a series of blunders that ends in victory. We certainly are making our fair share in this one.

Reaching the end of the access road, we enter a traffic circle connecting the access road to Highway 1. During busier times of the day, the radio would start to squawk identifying possible VBIED threats. Vehicle-borne improvised explosive device. During an earlier, simpler time I would have known them as car bombs—again, a term not nuanced or sophisticated enough for this thoroughly modern war. A car or truck can haul a lot of explosives. Amazingly deadly and, when driven by a suicidal fanatic, they become the Islamic equivalent of a Tomahawk missile. I pretend to have countermeasures against them, signs that say "stay back" in Dari. Too bad I am in a province that is both illiterate and only speaks Pashto. I am sure the Pashtun pride appreciates that the signs we use to tell them how to drive are in a language from Shiite Iran and spoken by their ancient enemies. If the indecipherable sign doesn't work, there is the universal language of pointing a .50-caliber machine gun at them. Hearts and minds. Of course, for an actual VBIED, none of these courses of actions is going to stop them. Really, I was only making sure to enrage the innocent. In Kandahar Province, pen flares were all the fashion. Better than a bullet and easy to see at night. There were minimal restrictions in the use of these pen flares, which are technically "nonlethal." I fired a few. One NCO in my old unit would fire twenty of them in a single convoy. They got him into the driver's seat and out of the gun turret pretty quickly, fortunately. I emphasize the "were" in minimal restrictions. Another PMT team embedded a burning flare into a kid's head. Skipping the "hearts" and going right for the "minds." The team swore it was a ricochet, but the flares don't move that quickly. That team had a reputation for stupid aggressiveness. The pen flare was worthless for all the same reasons as the sign. By the time I pulled out the pen flare and then went to my real weapon, the VBIED would be impaled on my bumper and would have exploded. Green lasers were another popular option. Flash them around on the hood, try to avoid the eyes. Right. Then there was the popular "drive down the middle of the road and make them pull over." Very popular with the locals. If I did this long enough, I got to see the spectacle of people crashing into ditches trying to avoid the twenty-ton armored vehicles going forty miles per hour down the middle of a two-lane road. Yet more hilarity. And nobody wears seatbelts, so probably painful, too. As bad as the Americans are, the Europeans are even worse. And their vehicles are bigger. The Canadians had even brought their seventy-ton main battle tanks. Just in case. All these techniques are borrowed from Iraq, where I figure they might have made sense. But they never made sense in Zabul, and so I ensure my teams don't use them. My teams share the roads with the civilian population and haven't fired a pen flare since I arrived. Haven't suffered any VBIEDs, either. Correlation doesn't equal causation, but I can say with certainty that I hadn't suffered by being a slightly friendlier neighbor. Friendly to a point. OK, probably not friendly, but at least not rude. It's a start. It is also a lot less stressful for me. I have enough problems as it is.

But this early in the morning, traffic is nonexistent. The lead vehicle (I am in the second) calls a simple "clear" over the net (network). I check the right side while the gunner and driver check the left. The BFT screen obscures the middle of the vehicle so the driver can't see to the right and I can't see to the left, so the TC becomes the eyes of the driver on his right side. The three-inch-thick glass and heavy pillars don't help visibility, either. The gunner has the best view but is the most exposed. Veering right, we finally join onto Highway 1. The traffic circle has an impressive, indeterminate monument in the middle with a small shack. A few police are there twenty-four hours a day, sleeping during the late night and early morning. I don't work much with the traffic police, arguably the bravest men in all Afghanistan. They wear distinctive white hats and are always alone or, at most, in pairs and are probably the most accessible representatives of the Afghan government. Perfect targets for Taliban in training. Not long ago, a traffic cop was killed in Kandahar

City. I always saw him when I was driving through the city. He looked about fifty (which, in Afghanistan, could mean thirty-five) and willing to stop an eighteen-wheeler going fifty miles per hour through sheer force of will. Shot down by a guy on a motorcycle. The only weapon the traffic cop carried was a homemade wooden baton. *Inshallah.* If Allah wills it. I don't see the traffic cops this early, but I know they are there in the shack, sipping tea if not sleeping. I get incessant complaints that the police, especially the traffic police, are shaking down drivers for cash at the dozen or so checkpoints along Highway 1 in Zabul. It is a constant battle. Ironically, good cops get more complaints than bad cops because a good cop causes trouble for the wrong people. The Afghans know that the naïve Americans will believe anything. What is easier than filing a complaint against a good cop so the Americans push to get him removed? But a bad cop will beat somebody's ass, so the Afghans have to be more careful should they dare complain about a really bad cop. I've gotten a couple of corrupt ones removed. "Removed" is a nice euphemism. No one is ever fired, just moved around from one district to another. Kind of like the provincial governor. But I can never be sure whether I am doing the right thing or getting played. Afghans don't completely understand the nuances of Afghanistan politics, so why should I think I'm going to figure them out?

Accelerating down the road, we swerve left only 200 meters later and pass through the first of two gates entering the Zabul provincial ANP headquarters. The road parallels Highway 1 and the wall to the compound. Between the access road and the highway was a series of Hesco bastions: the same kind of 500-gallon fabric cubes lined with mesh and holding dirt that were also part of the chicane in the ANA camp. A giant sandbag for a more mechanized age. Hesco bastions surround all FOBs that don't have concrete walls. Mostly they are simply called "Hescos." They will stop pretty much anything and are easy to erect and fill. I first saw them in Macedonia fifteen years earlier and noted what a good idea they were. I wish I had bought stock then. They are everywhere. Abandoned ones are stolen and used for storing material. They are used as dams to save floodwaters for irrigation. I can find them on the highway acting as speed bumps or substitute chicanes. They probably number in the millions between Iraq and Afghanistan. They are literally lifesavers. A VBIED went off at the gate to the PHQ before I arrived in Afghanistan, and the concrete wall suffered some damage. My predecessor secured enough Hescos to build a secondary wall protecting the PHQ. Defense in depth.

Between the access road and the PHQ is a rose garden. The Afghans have an amazing affinity for gardens. Maybe not so amazing considering the mostly desert landscape they live in. The rosebushes line the entranceway. Some of them are sickly, but some bloom beautifully. This garden is about half the size of a football field, maybe eighty by thirty meters. The first gate I passed through was a hastily erected one as a result of the VBIED, but the main gate through the main wall has a magnificent archway with an inscription. Funny, because maybe ten percent of the police can actually read it. Whether it is Koranic or secular I can't tell; visually, Arabic and Dari look the same to the untrained eye. Since the PHQ dates to the Soviet occupation and was built under their watchful eyes, I suspect the language is secular. The guards smile as they lift the vehicle barrier. *They* won't be going out today.

Because it is early, the compound is largely deserted. There are several unfinished buildings in various states of disrepair. Contracts were let out to build barracks and offices. The Americans pay well and up front, which usually means a verification of fifty percent completed construction will get full payment. Twice the contractor has built to fifty percent, taken the full payment, and then left the buildings incomplete. Again, Afghan humor. The concrete is all hand mixed and of horrible quality. The rebar—the steel reinforcing rod—is about a third of what should be used, especially in a seismically active country. The older buildings date to the eighties when the Soviets were throwing money at Afghanistan. I'll say this for the Soviets: Nobody skipped out halfway through construction when they paid. The buildings built then are all sturdy, if ugly.

The compound consists of a citadel-type tower on the south side with another garden. Going clockwise around from there I see a partially completed office and the main gate office. Then a mosque, which is the largest completed building in the compound. After the mosque is yet another rose garden and then the main headquarters building. Here is where the commanding officer, Brigadier General Sarjang, eats and sleeps. His family remains in Kabul, where they are relatively safe. His oldest son, however, is a new lieutenant in the police force and he is assigned in the MacArthur tradition with his father in Zabul. The officers' dining room is also in that building. The Afghans throw a great dinner party, and Sarjang's was the best I have attended since being in Afghanistan. Better than the provincial governor's and better than his nominal boss's in Kandahar.

In front of the headquarters building there is a patio where the general holds court in the mornings and evenings. In the Soviet and Afghan tradition, the general micromanages almost everything. Everything of importance, and much that isn't, must be signed by him. So some mornings he spends about two hours signing the various documents while his staff sits and chats, sipping tea. During the heat of the day, he moves indoors to his office. The stucco-covered concrete is quite cooling, and he even has an air conditioner, which he rarely uses. The furniture is all overstuffed and baroque, unlike the modern stuff generally seen in American offices. Much of the day-to-day mentorship consists of me simply being in the same office as this general while he does his work. I say little and understand even less. At the end of the day, I will ask my terp what was going on. Occasionally the general will ask for my advice, mostly out of politeness. The facts are: I am not a cop, I am not a general, and I am not an Afghan. So telling an Afghan cop who is a general how to do his business is pretty hypocritical.

Continuing the rotating tour of the provincial headquarters, there is a barracks with a bakery and, finally, another unfinished three-story building. ANP green Rangers—about twenty of them, mostly new—are parked in front of the citadel in a covered area with a concrete pad. The whole compound is probably about three acres.

Our vehicles swing around to face the exit, and people start to get out of the trucks. Ordinarily the jammers would be turned off, but we want to make sure no phone calls go out before we leave. Anyone we tell the mission to (except the general) is coming with us. That's the theory, at least. It probably wouldn't work for an intelligent Taliban spy, but it will for a cop who just wants to call his brother. The turret-mounted machine guns on the trucks stay loaded. We won't be here long.

I head toward the general's office while the rest of the soldiers head off to the bakery to grab the fresh *naan* (Afghan flatbread). The naan is made all day long and is an accompaniment to all meals. After about five hours it gets stale, but when it's fresh it's marvelous. Naan can get a little boring by itself, so my family sent me some jams and honeys to spread onto it, which gives it a nice, sweet variety. Also a nice touch with lamb kabobs. In the hinterlands, the naan is a different story. Once while on foot chasing Taliban deep in a valley to the north of Qalat, I stumbled upon a Kuchi tent. Feeling tired, and knowing I wasn't going to catch them, I stopped to say "hi." The family consisted of a man who looked fifty but was probably thirty, as well as his two wives and five or so kids (that I could see). There were two tents: one for the family and one for the selected livestock. One of the wives had just baked some naan and the gentleman offered my terp and me some. It was horrible. Of course, I ate it all. I felt terrible taking bread from the man who had so little in life, but it would have insulted him horribly had I refused. I paid for it later, however: the Afghan diet plan basically consists of crapping every sixty minutes for a few days. Just perfect when on a mission in a HMMWV. But at the time, I didn't know that was going to happen and felt like I had stepped back a few centuries. I asked the terp to ask the man if he had ever seen an American before. The guy replied he had never seen a foreigner before. I felt like Buzz Aldrin with body armor. Charting new territory.

Here at PHQ, somebody hands me a piece of naan that is still hot to the touch. It is great. The morning is cool and clear, and I check out the garden to assess the sickly roses. My mom kept roses that were quite a bit nicer, but I think it is tougher to do here. Soldiers constantly tend to the flowers during the day, watering them by hand with a bucket. I don't see bees very often, but they must be there somewhere.

General Sarjang comes out, obviously newly awakened. He doesn't seem upset but a bit surprised. We sit together on the patio and tea is quickly brought. *Singeh, jureh, pachaitai.* The Pashto greeting is quickly exchanged with smiling faces. The chai boy leaves, and the two of us sit alone and quietly together for a few minutes. After the expected silence to enjoy the tea, I tell Sarjang I am going to Surkhagan. He smiles and chuckles. I then ask him where his deputy, Julani, is. Sarjang is a fighter, I don't doubt this. He has literally stripped his sleeves and shown his scars. But he isn't a fighter anymore; Julani is the hatchet man in the organization.

Julani's life story is an interesting mix. He is one of the few Tajiks in the police force in Zabul. He is also from Farah, a traditionally Pashtun area. He has been assigned to Zabul on and off since 1989. He sports a neatly trimmed beard, whereas Sarjang, the Pashtun, has only a thick mustache. As thin as Sarjang is husky, Julani exudes the confidence and quick smile of a fighter. He is also vicious. I have not seen but have heard the stories of him beating his own policemen with his radio for failing to show proper respect. Once, while walking downtown in Qalat, a young man failed to show respect to a *baba* (elder) in Julani's presence. The young man, too, was beaten mercilessly.

Julani carries a US-issue M9 pistol that he claims was given to him by Special Forces (SF). Yeah, right. Somebody got their ass chewed for that one. I dare not question him about it, though. Julani is a fighter and I need fighters. Twice Julani has gone out with us on missions and both times we made contact with Taliban and killed some. He is my good luck charm, and I look forward to having him with me during today's fight.

But Julani isn't here.

Sarjang informs me that he went south to Tarnak Wa Jaldak. Tarnak Wa Jaldak is halfway between Qalat and Kandahar. Lots of problems there with the local police chief shaking down drivers at checkpoints. My team leader down there has worked hard and somewhat successfully trying to stop it. Julani is there for a good reason, I hope. Nothing I can do.

I ask Sarjang for thirty guys with a good commander. He tells me he has just the man: Shah Khan. Not sure how he earned the sobriquet of "Khan." Khan means a lot of things in Afghanistan. For some, it simply indicates that the bearer is of Pathan (Pashtun) descent. For others, it is the title earned as a warlord. Julani is known more formally as Julani Khan, despite the fact he is a Tajik. Shah Khan is nominally the police chief for the district of Khaki Afghan, where there are no police. That's the slot he holds—and the pay he collects. I have never worked with him before nor have I ever heard of him. He is tall and about thirty. His mouth hangs open a bit, which makes him look stupid. He also says nothing and his eyes dart around. Not a good sign. He is accompanied everywhere by a slightly older guy, whose rank indicates private. Shorter and stronger, he looks sharp. I call him "Mahmoud" by default. He may be the de facto commander, which happens often. Family influence, reputation, or any other of several factors may make someone the actual commander in lieu of the de jure commander. We meet up and start talking about what is going to go on today. But not everything.

I pull out the map and show them what I am planning on doing. Siar is there as interpreter. I show them the Dab Pass and say, *"Sahbaz Khel."* Shah Khan nods his head, indicating he knows the area or is at least pretending to. I tell them I want to check out the village and say "hi." Just a regular presence patrol. Meet and greet in another parlance. Although I told Sarjang the truth, I hope he doesn't share that truth with Mahmoud or Shah Khan. He probably won't. These guys aren't his first team. Plus, he probably doesn't think the plan will work. I didn't tell Sarjang about the ISR or the Apaches. Can't share everything. You can't completely trust anybody. He'll know by tonight.

I leave Gregory and Geno to talk to the police and try to figure out why Julani isn't around. I asked specifically for Julani for today's mission and usually Sarjang will support that. Sarjang seems a bit abrupt, and I wonder if he is upset that I was questioning him. Hell, it is an early morning for both of us. He is probably just tired. Regardless, not having Julani is nagging at me. Again, nothing I can do about it, but the fact does not escape me that I have *never* made contact with the Taliban without him.

Julani has been in Zabul for twenty years. He knows everybody and everything about the province. In an earlier mission when my team killed a top commander, Julani instantly identified him. "How do you know?" I asked. Julani just smiled. Maybe he fought with him against the Russians. Maybe he fought with him *with* the Russians. Maybe they had dinner together last week. I don't know *how* he knows, but I do know that he is right. During that same fight, he was talking on a captured Taliban ICOM radio. He was addressing the Taliban on the other end by name, taunting him to come and get the commander we (the Americans) were peeing on. Of course we weren't, but the Taliban didn't know that. Julani was loving every minute of it. Now, Julani will get me into a fight, but that doesn't mean he is going to be doing any fighting. He is no fool and he has enough of his own scars, proving he has nothing to prove. He will come up after the ANP and I have finished firing. Not long after, however—maybe a minute or two, just being on the scene, providing the muscle, the intimidation factor, and the eyes and ears of the palace-bound general. If Sarjang is the emperor, Julani is his Darth Vader.

Sarjang doesn't remind me of the emperor from *Star Wars,* however. He does remind me of Jabba the Hutt. Holding court, surrounded by minions and minstrels, eating well, and enjoying his role of king of his kingdom. He is a big guy: plump, but not fat. His laugh has a deep bass that is reminiscent of the character in the movie. The dusky office with the well-padded furniture adds to the image of Jabba's palace from the movie, along with the gates to the palace, surrounded by his guards, as skinny as the pig-like guards in *Return of the Jedi* were fat. Afghanistan often reminds me of *Star Wars* in one way or another. Kandahar Airfield (KAF) is equivalent to the Mos Eisley spaceport from the movie, with soldiers from thirty different countries in different uniforms speaking different languages. The boardwalk and Dutch Café provide the ambiance of the cantina scene. Everybody armed. At KAF, as in the Mos Eisley spaceport, I see aircraft from every possible country and era taking off and landing incessantly. It, too, appears as the only way in or out. Certainly, the terrain reminds me of the Tunisian desert where the movie was filmed. The Baluchi wastelands have the rolling dunes, there are mountains enough to provide that bit of similarity, and the plains of Zabul provide ample examples of the dirt farmers scratching out a living in the form of Luke Skywalker's Uncle

Owen and Aunt Beru. The mud huts lack the computerized cookware, but the building material is identical.

The people fit the role as well. The children surrounding us and begging for food are Jawas. In the words of C-3PO, "disgusting creatures." And the Taliban, of course, are the Sand People: raiders who flee when threatened but attack if they find the target defenseless. Unfortunately, I know all too well that the US forces are perceived as the imperial stormtroopers, in our armor, randomly stopping vehicles and searching constantly for unidentifiable phantoms. We don't slaughter Jawas, however much the Taliban like to say we do. And like the Empire in the movie, we are chasing someone not from the land we are in. Not sure if George Lucas was just creative, or actually took a vacation to Afghanistan at some point. But no matter what, he sure nailed Afghanistan, even if he didn't mean to.

While I am talking with Sarjang, Shah Khan is assembling his men and getting them sorted into the ANP's green Rangers. While badged "Ford," they were actually made in Taiwan. The small diesel-driven four-door trucks have a light bar across the top and a roll cage in the bed, usually mounting a PKM medium machine gun. Four ANP will ride in the cab of the truck while another two to four will ride in the back. I have occasionally driven them around the FOB. Sometimes in KAF I would borrow the token ANP Ranger that accompanied us to do errands. Much less cumbersome than the twenty- to thirty-ton MRAPs I usually took to get to KAF. Great little trucks that easily break but are easily fixed. Not the best for out here, but good enough. The National Directorate of Security (NDS) troopers get the much better and preferred Toyota HiLux trucks with a snazzy paint job. ANA have tan Rangers, in the two-door model. However, they will generally avoid using those for their new UAHs.

The Afghans differentiate themselves in even more ways than their vehicles; they have borrowed the American proclivity for different uniforms for different units. The police run in a cheap gray polyester (exchanged for cheap gray wool in winter). The army has battle dress uniforms (BDUs) in the traditional woodland pattern: green, black, and brown. The Afghan border patrol has what is known as the "chocolate chip" pattern: mostly cream with black spots and waves of tans and browns. For where I am, the border patrol's uniform is probably the best. The private security guards who guard the governor run with a ripped-off version of the new marine digital woodland pattern—the same three colors of the BDU except in a pixilated pattern borrowed from the Canadians—itself a derivative of what was known as *flektarn* camouflage worn by the Nazis in World War II. The NDS run in what they feel like, but if they do choose a uniform, it is usually a solid olive drab much like those worn by the US Army in Vietnam. I need not worry as there will be only three uniforms where I am going today. My own ACU, the gray of the ANP, and the traditional civilian dress shared by both the Taliban and the civilians they mingle with.

After twenty minutes of shouting, searching, and sighing, the ANP are finally lined up. Two of their trucks are in the lead, each with about five police. Then Gregory's UAH, another ANP Ranger, my HMMWV, another Ranger, Geno's HMMWV, and an ANP Ranger bringing up the rear. With my terp Siar, I grab Geno, Gregory, Shah Khan, and Mahmoud and confirm they know we are going to the Dab Pass and then to Shabazkehl. Gregory and Geno share a smirking glance, knowing our true destination. The heads nod up and down. So off to the valley of death with ANP I don't know and have never worked with.

I shout, "Mount up!" and the US guys scramble with their body armor and helmets while the not-so-heavily-attired ANP look on in either envy or pity. The gunners climb over the tops of the vehicles and lower themselves down. A seat belt extends from the floor to ensure that if we roll over, the gunners won't be thrown out and crushed. There is debate whether it is better to be thrown clear of a possible fire (and ensuing conflagration from all the ammunition and explosives contained in the vehicles) or take your chances with the rollover. I haven't seen a case where being thrown clear saved somebody's life, but a gunner died after being thrown from a truck while everyone else lived. So the gunner restraints are worn—yet another of my many unpopular orders. The TC or driver usually hands up the seat belt to the gunner, who can't see his feet particularly well. I hand Dhakal's to him and he attaches himself with a D-ring to his belt, which is heavily reinforced to act as a hasty harness. Through my radio headset, I hear the radio burst to life yet again as checks are heard coming across. I contact Zabul Base on the radio and let them know we are leaving PHQ. I send a BFT message to the HQ in KAF and share that info with my immediate headquarters, which is a three-hour drive to the south outside Kandahar City in FOB Walton. The same message is sent to Rob, whose nearly immediate reply indicates he is already in the TOC, where he will stay all day during the fight. I guess he didn't fall back to sleep.

Shah Khan is in the lead truck, which starts to move; the rest all follow. Eight trucks go out in a row through the same gate we entered a half hour ago. Sarjang stands at the gate waving a farewell to us all. In three months, I have never seen him do that before. That particularly unique gesture perplexes me, but I quickly let it go as I again focus ahead on the upcoming mission.

IF:THEN, IF:THEN, IF:THEN.

3

MOVEMENT TO CONTACT

0615.

The real mission starts. The radio briefly confirms that all the vehicles are still jammin' with weapons hot. The convoy turns back toward the traffic circle. The pace of the convoy has quickened as the ANP drive their Rangers with the reckless abandon of teenagers in rental cars combined with third-world driving laws. The US drivers struggle to maintain contact with the lead vehicles. That's why it is important to have the Rangers interspaced with the US vehicles while ensuring we never take the lead. The ANP serve as ad hoc mine rollers with men inside.

I filled this role once before during a different mission in Surkhagan, but that was after the ANP had already hit one IED. They had done their bit, and because I had only been in Zabul a few weeks, it was important to prove to them I was willing to share the risk. My driver then, a young, out-of-shape private, was visibly terrified for the first few miles as he weaved erratically, looking for the least trafficable route in a *wadi*, or ravine, covered with IEDs. Our vehicle was filled with horrible jokes and nervous laughter. The wadi was filled with camels, more than usual. That and thirty vehicles of ANP, Romanians, special forces, and explosive ordinance disposal (EOD) teams from the navy, trying desperately to follow our tire marks exactly. Ironically, I have never seen a lead vehicle hit an IED. Always the second or third. Yet no one wants to be the lead, regardless of statistical safety. Later I learned how to navigate cross-country and avoid the wadis when I had to.

At the traffic circle we veer right and away from the castle and safety of the FOB. We are driving down the new main market road. There is a large trench dug along it, a primitive start to a fledgling sewer system that will be, for the first time in Zabul, below ground. Despite this attempt at modern living, the buildings lining the sides of the road are still made of mud. The shops haven't opened yet. There are two motorcycle dealers;

Taliban are probably eighty percent of their business. Then cheap Chinese trinket shops with open-air butchers. From time to time, there are some stands that sell vegetables of varying quality. The chai shop and rug merchants. Julani and I occasionally stroll through the market and take in the various wares and aromas. Julani's drink of choice is the addicting and potent Red Bull original. The most intoxicating aspect of it is a powerful extract of nicotine. I had one, once. The jitters of a two-pot-a-day coffee habit pale in comparison to one can of this stuff. Julani downs them while he smokes. He knows everyone in the marketplace and they all know Julani. They hasten to be the first to offer a drink or a shady place to chat. During the heat of the day, Julani and I once sat for two hours while he talked and I listened. The children were napping, but would occasionally awake and look in awe, smiling shyly, at the American in their midst. I gave some Afghani (the currency of Afghanistan) to my terp, Highlander, to buy some candy and hand it out. The kids were hesitant to accept it, but the baba said it was "OK" and they greedily grabbed it. Maybe this is what counterinsurgency (COIN) is about. I hope that in ten years, because of a single act of charity, the kid decides not to blow up a UAH. Who knows? Julani repeats this act in every town we go to in Zabul and is always met with the same level of familiarity from the locals. But Sarjang isn't. Let there be no doubt that Sarjang is in command, but Julani is definitely the face of the police in Zabul.

The market is only about a hundred meters on this stretch of road. We pass by the local girls' school with the permanent police detachment next to it. Guarding an all-girls' school might be the most dangerous job in Zabul. Schools and teachers of all types are a favorite target of the Taliban, but girls' schools enjoy an unfortunately earned reputation as the Taliban's favorite place to strew terror. In Kandahar, a girl had strong acid thrown in her face as she left school one day. To add to the inflammatory mix, some of the older girls dispense with the traditional, all-encompassing burka and wear a simple *hijab*, or scarf, over their hair. In the United States, a girl wearing a full dress, with sleeves past the arms and a scarf around her neck and hair showing only her face would be the model of piety. In Afghanistan, it's the equivalent of Lady Gaga in a thong. In terms of personal risk, it is also the equivalent of storming Omaha Beach. These girls are taking the strongest stand imaginable in this society against the Taliban. If we fail at our mission as a whole, they will be killed at the first opportunity. We often drive by after school is out with all the children walking home, most with a male escort of some kind. Despite the fact that the school and the students attending it are in existence because of the United States, not a single hand is waving. There is no acknowledgment of the Americans' existence by any girl past the age of eight. *It's not hatred, I think; it is modesty.* At least that's what I tell myself.

A quick left at the girls' school and we are hemmed in by mud-walled family compounds guarded by large metal gates on both sides of the roads. Even in a metropolis such as Qalat, the compounds contain the same mix of barnyard and cooking areas. The walls themselves are six to twelve inches thick and capable of stopping any type of bullet. Even a rocket-propelled grenade (RPG) will only create a small hole. Outside of large cities, many girls past the age of ten will leave those walls only once a year, at most. When they do so, nearly all of them will still be enclosed in the mandatory blue burkas.

I have been in these compounds dozens of times with the ANP. None have electricity. We can go from blinding sunlight to smoky darkness instantly. The cumbersome flashlight attached to my rifle is the only way to cut the gloom. The ANP search meticulously and destructively. I always feel bad for the families, but the ANP almost inevitably find evidence of Taliban when they search. Can we "turn" a family who already has several members in the Taliban? Are the families here so intertwined that even a pro-government family will inevitably have a son or nephew or cousin in the Taliban, regardless? Given the corruption of the Afghan government and disdain the government has for the people of Zabul, could any of them be pro-government? These questions always are in the back of my mind as I work with the police. I try to ensure that despite the heavy-handed searches, the ANP don't steal anything. That's the least I can do.

In just five minutes we have progressed past the actual city limits of Qalat and find ourselves in the suburban orchards that ring the city on both sides of the Tarnak River. A few weeks previously, a local farmer found an IED in the trees along this same road. The type he found is an especially vicious type of canister shot. The explosives are packed with large ball bearings in the front. When fired, it sends a hailstorm of metal in a ninety-degree arc toward the road. While these IEDs won't penetrate HMMWV armor, they will possibly kill a gunner and can literally shred an ANP Ranger, as I have seen twice so far. About a dozen police have been killed by these IEDs along the orchards on Highway 1 in the past few weeks, but this was the first one reported off the main road. Due to their homemade nature, they can fail to detonate. By the same token, you may not know exactly when they may go off. I would normally wait for EOD to deal with the problem, but EOD won't come unless US or coalition forces are on site—sometimes not even then. By the time my soldiers got there, the ANP were already taking it apart. Not the smartest move, but it did take care of the problem.

The orchards themselves are mostly almond trees. The almond tree is one of the few species that prospers in the deserts of Afghanistan. The almonds they produce are a constant snacking item. They're good raw or roasted and are often coated in a thick sugar frosting, which makes them deliciously addicting. Sarjang knows I enjoy them, so he always has extra out after we arrive, along with tea. Despite the hardiness of the trees, they wouldn't grow without the Tarnak River. A raging flood in the spring and a muddy trickle in the summer, the Tarnak still poses a significant barrier between Highway 1 and the eastern half of Zabul Province. Regardless of the flow of water, the five-meter vertical banks are impassible in all but about a dozen places throughout the province. Ordinarily the Taliban might put IEDs in these crossing points, but they are critical for everyone to use and the Taliban doesn't want to piss off the population much more than we do without good justification. Plus, the Taliban like to go to the market as much as anybody else. The bridge at Qalat is the only all-weather bridge across the Tarnak. A monument to modernity in an otherwise ancient landscape. The steel truss construction looks recent, possibly post 9/11. I don't know and haven't asked, but I am happy it is there. My teams to the north and south, Nomad and Viper respectively, can't cross the Tarnak any time but summer and fall and therefore lose access to the eastern (and more Taliban) parts of their districts. This time of year, the access is nearly unlimited for both the Taliban and ANP. Hence the expression, "the fighting season."

Across the bridge, the road stretches level and smooth to the east. It's too bad we can't drive on it. The new road is being built to support a new "super FOB" off Highway 1, FOB Wolverine. This FOB is to play host to the incoming 2nd Infantry Division and their computerized Stryker infantry fighting vehicles. These vehicles, it is hoped, will provide the high-tech communications required to make decisive operations against the Taliban a regular occurrence in Zabul. Since they will be permanently on the eastern side of the Tarnak, they will have more freedom of movement. But bigger vehicles and more soldiers mean a greatly increased logistics footprint, which will require a paved road in addition to a brand new airfield, capable of handling C-17s. All these decisions were made against the best advice of the provincial reconstruction team, battlespace owner, and Afghan forces. But the ANP was a strong supporter. This is probably because the logistics officer for the ANP moonlights as the largest contractor in Zabul and he got millions to build the road. Which job is permanent and which one is the moonlighting job is open to honest debate. The fact is that Malik, the logistics officer, has juice. Too much juice. In order to do the amount of contracting work he does in Zabul, he is making deals with Taliban. Guaranteed. Whether those deals extend to security issues is unknown. His deals aren't that good, however, because that beautiful stretch of road I see before me is assumed to be strewn with IEDs. So we are going to "handrail" the road for the next fifty kilometers, driving next to, but not on, the road. The frustration is palpable. This would be a forty-minute drive if we could take the road. Instead, it's four hours at a creeping pace. At least it is safe—somewhat.

Occasionally we have to veer off and drive on the actual road to cross a wadi. At this point, an ANP will jump out of the back of his Ranger and do a quick visual scan. The ANP aren't deemed worthy of metal detectors quite yet. And, in the brilliance of the military assistance, they will be getting $10,000 top-of-the line units, whereas a beachcombers' special for $300 would actually be better. The United States has fairly biblical notions in some regards; as man was made in the image of God, so shall the ANSF (Afghan National Security Forces) be made in the image of the US military.

This Kabuki dance/Chinese fire drill is repeated about every kilometer. And we have so many more to go. There is always a tradeoff between dismounting and hoping the eye is sharper than the IED, and trying to go cross-country through the innumerable wadis and washouts. For every two or three dismounts to check for IEDs, the ANP get stuck trying to avoid the main road. Here the issue takes a little longer and is always more humorous. The ANP Rangers are equipped with a fairly nice winch, which is used for everything. So one winch will be attached to another ANP Ranger, which sometimes holds and sometimes doesn't. Allah help them if the cable snaps, because there are always ten ANP standing right around the cable during these ad hoc adventures in vehicle recovery. The winch takes time, however. If the stuck vehicle seems to be on the verge of freedom, those same ten ANP just come together to push and shove through the problem. Fortunately, the UAH, despite its weight, can go anywhere a Ranger can. So as long as the ANP are leading the way, I don't have to worry about being stuck. Which, at 14,000 pounds, is a good thing. The exception is in muddy areas. The lightweight Ranger will float across mud that will mire a UAH. And a stuck UAH in the mud is a PITA (pain in the ass). It is June, and mud isn't a problem once we get across the Tarnak. It hasn't rained since April.

Fortunately, these problems don't affect us too much, other than lengthening our day. The clock hasn't started. The UAV hasn't detected any undue movement from the Taliban in the village of Abdul Qadir Kalay. As long as the patrol looks like a movement toward the Dab Pass, the Taliban in the Surkhagan Valley (where Abdul Qadir Kalay is) shouldn't react. I am positive that every Taliban in a 100-mile radius is aware of my patrol. But as long as they don't know about the UAV and our true destination, the clock doesn't start.

We continue the leisurely journey to the southeast and toward FOB Wolverine. There are Taliban all over this area, but they generally operate in smaller groups. Legend has it the district police chief in Suri District, which we've crossed into, is either Taliban or willfully ignorant of Taliban activities. The Suri Taliban are a bit more mercenary in their approach. Rather than taking the jihad to the infidels, they occupy their time with shakedowns and intimidation of the local population. Leaving these Taliban alone is actually the better alternative. Already one group was expelled forcefully by the locals, and their continued poor behavior is turning the locals against the Taliban without any help from the ISAF or ANSF. If only all Taliban were so stupid. Yet, they are also smart enough not to attack ISAF/ANSF too brazenly. This disjointed nature of operations shows that the provincial shadow governor (the Taliban chief of Zabul) doesn't have very good control of his various factions. If he did, they would all be behaving in a more uniform manner. The rumor continues that the contractor for the road (again, the provincial ANP logistics officer, Malik) is paying the Taliban not to attack his workers. This is almost assuredly true, as the road will provide a logistical artery into the expanding FOB. It benefits the coalition and hurts the Taliban. In the absence of payoff, the workers would be attacked unendingly. However, the payoff doesn't extend to not planting IEDs along the improving route. We all must live within our budget, and let's face it, IEDs are good business. The contractor gets paid to build the road and also receives a guaranteed stream of income to repair it from the inevitable craters. Plus, every IED is a change document that delays the project and results in additional charges to the government. In chaos, there is profit. In extreme chaos, there is extreme profit. And for triple-distilled chaos, Zabul is tough to beat.

As we amble along, the rough route provides at least a few advantages. Since we are breaking new ground and moving so slowly, the dust is manageable. This late after the rains, the heavily travelled dirt roads we so carefully avoid quickly become a dust bowl. The fine "moon dust" settles on the side of the trails while the heavier and larger sand drops quickly back down. The more travelled routes will have six to twelve inches of talcum-like dust that envelops my feet when I get out. This dust is also easily used as camouflage, making identification of IEDs that much more difficult. So while our vehicles here are only about ten meters apart, the distance will stretch to 100 to 200 meters on a more frequently travelled route. This makes following in the lead vehicles' tire tracks all the more difficult. Time remains on our side, so the slow, boring journey fits my needs quite nicely.

Sergeant Dhakal, his thick Nepalese accent muffled by the sound of the HMMWV's engine coming across the turret, asks the obvious question, "Sir, you sure we are going to find Taliban?"

"We already have found them. The question is whether we can get there in time to kill them."

"Well?"

"I don't know. If we get the Apaches and we don't tip them off when we swing north to Dab, either the Apaches will kill them, or we will."

Moore, focused on the driving, asks the more pointed question, "How long is that going to take?"

"Two more hours to Dab. Two hours in Shabazkehl. One hour to Surkhagan. Pick up the pieces after that. Four hours to exfil."

"Shit."

"Yep. Let's just not get blown up. You did fill up the gas cans, right?"

"Yeah, both of them."

"Good, we are going to need them. Anything to see up there, Sergeant?"

"ANP are stuck again."

"Great. If you shoot something, let me know."

"Deal."

The UAH settles into quiet again as the driver and gunner remain occupied and I fiddle with the BFT.

"Any change?" I text to Zabul Base.

"Neg. TB still at OBJ. No movement."

"How many?"

"Twenty."

This is the motorcycle count, as it's the only thing the UAV can see. The Taliban are inside the various structures. So there are at least twenty Taliban with a max of forty. Well, thirty-nine; the commander will always have his own motorcycle.

"THX."

The radio from the other trucks is quiet. Siar is in back so I figure I should check on him as well.

"Siar, anything on the ICOM?"

"No, Sir. All quiet."

"Thanks. Let me know."

"I will. I want to kill some motherfucking Taliban today."

"Don't we all?"

And that is that. I settle again into my thoughts as the HMMWV bounces along. Prior to the Apaches arriving in Zabul, there was no way to get on top of the Taliban. The Task Force Zabul LNO (liaison officer), Greg Cannata, and I would talk about our frustration with responding to the Taliban attacks. Find, fix, and destroy. That's the troika of success in maneuver, kinetic warfare ("kinetic" being the new euphemism for "killing"). We could find them when they attacked and we could destroy them. We couldn't fix them. Fix, in warrior speak, means to hold them in place. In the movie *Patton,* George C. Scott eloquently paraphrased, "You hold on to 'em by the nose, and kick 'em in the ass." A standard mentored ANP patrol had plenty of ass kicking. ANP Rangers can't run down Taliban on motorcycles, but an Apache can. But then the Apaches are limited: They have a hard time seeing someone in the warm desert if he doesn't move. Plus, they can't verify whether it's a bad guy or not unless they see a weapon. So if the Taliban go to ground and hide under a tree, a wall, or even their own turbans, the Apaches can't do anything about it. But the ANP can, *if* we can get there in time. And with the unblinking eye of the ISR circling sixty kilometers to the north, we didn't even have to wait for them to attack.

I feel bad for Greg. He is a regular infantry type and a Notre Dame alum (and fanatic). This wasn't supposed to be his tour, but his predecessor was killed in an IED strike. So Greg got pulled to replace him, as the LNO slot is tagged on a single battalion in Germany. But the deal was nothing outside of the wire. While he would like to have been on this trip as the fruition of both of our schemes and wishes, he is stuck watching the BFT and running around his FOB, FOB Lagman. And I frankly don't know what is going to happen. The Apaches may not take off, in which case this will be a giant waste of time. Or they may take off and not engage, whereas the Taliban will happily drive off into the mountains before we can do anything. If nothing else, I am not in the tactical operations center (TOC) all day answering email. Small victories still count.

After three hours of minimal chitchat and increasingly sore asses, we reach the left turn toward Dab. Only a few kilometers away is the fairly large base at Wolverine, which is slated to become much larger in the near future. Being stationed here would put us within ten minutes of some of the best Taliban hunting in Afghanistan, but the base is all ANA, so no such luck. Rob was on one mission with Swampfox, and the TOC at Wolverine sent a testy BFT message: "What is Swampfox doing here?"

I answered back, "Killing Taliban, look into it." This did little to improve relationships between the police and army mentors. But the facts were that Swampfox got into a TIC (troops in contact) only six kilometers from Wolverine. If the Taliban is that close to your base and you aren't doing anything about it, you have some problems you need to address.

It is still a little before 0800, and the route takes us north by northeast, paralleling the Sur Ghar mountain chain that separates the central part of Zabul from the eastern part. The going becomes much slower and rougher. The water runs off the mountains, so while we were previously running roughly alongside the innumerable wadis, we are now running perpendicular to them.

During this crawl Dhakal calls out, "Sir, got some guys with AKs walking about 500 meters to our three o'clock."

I verify the information and relay it to the other HMMWVs. Yep, civilians with AKs on a morning jaunt. They have a Toyota HiLux (the preferred mode of transportation for all Afghans, including Taliban) trailing behind them. They are looking at us and we are looking at them. Taliban aren't usually so bold; this doesn't make sense. They are walking the road from the Suri district capital to the Dab Pass. A favored place for IEDs. Are they planting IEDs? During the day? Taliban hide their guns; they don't show them in the open.

"Siar, what the fuck is going on?"

"I don't know, Sir. But they aren't Taliban."

And that settles it. On the word of a twenty-two-year-old interpreter, we don't shoot. As our driving pace roughly mirrored their walking pace, the ANP are able to eventually figure out these men worked for the road construction company that had a contract to improve the dirt road through Dab. Every morning they sweep the road for new IEDs and have to provide their own security to do so. Good guys. Well, that was somewhat reassuring, but not really since I didn't know it beforehand. This is not your standard war. "Shoot first and ask questions later" is no longer an acceptable course of action.

We are currently operating in what is known as a "weapons tight" status. There are three statuses: hold, tight, and free. A hold status means, "Engage only in self-defense." Basically, do not fire until fired upon or until directly threatened. A tight status means, "Engage if target is positively identified as enemy." And free means, "Engage anything not positively identified as friendly." This would be the "kill 'em all, let Allah sort them out" school of COIN. Needless to say, weapons free doesn't happen very often. Tight is the standard. But there is no torque wrench for COIN, so how tight "tight" is has yet to be agreed upon.

Positive identification (PID). That is the buzzword—or phrase, really. It's the difference between living and dying, killing or not killing, shoot or don't shoot. Now, what constitutes PID is often changing and always debated. Some say a vehicle that doesn't pull over is PID for a possible suicide attack. Some say PID means a weapon pointed at you. But sometimes it's hard to tell. Civilians walking around with AK-47s could easily be construed as PID, but I also have to take into account their actions. *Yeah, they were civilians with guns, but they weren't acting like Taliban.* But then I can PID somebody on a road without a gun. The Afghans know better than we do who is Taliban and who isn't, and their calculation generally has nothing to do with weapons. Just one of the many benefits of doing missions with the ANP. They are rarely wrong, and when they are, that's their problem, not mine.

I am only a couple of klicks (kilometers) away from the mountains, so while there are a lot of wadis, they haven't combined to form insurmountable obstacles. The vehicles aren't getting stuck as often and the pace is more even, if slower.

The UAH is filled with a slight fog of fine dust. Having been on his feet for three hours while wearing fifty pounds of armor and kit, Dhakal shifts more often, trying to take the weight off. He weighs only 130 or so pounds in the first place. The early morning naan is wearing off, so I grab some jerky and start munching. The dust gets to the jerky before I do, however. *Oh, well.*

We pass a Kuchi camp being broken down, its inhabitants preparing to move to the next desolate stretch of desert that no one else wants to live in. The camels that usually wander about grazing are being loaded with the tents and the few material possessions that don't walk on their own. A donkey is hobbled by a short piece of rope to ensure it doesn't wander off. A few of the kids will probably ride that. Camels, according to their nature, stay close by and I have never seen one tethered, even when it's not in use. But it is rare to see a donkey on its own untethered or otherwise hobbled. Usually two legs are tied together, and the pitiful creature hops and hobbles around attempting to find a scrub of grass to eat. An apt mascot for Afghanistan. Despite my presence squarely on the Asian continent, the camels are of the one-hump Arabian variety. I almost never see them being used for anything. This is the first time I have seen them actually loaded up with gear. They are as much an Afghan equivalent of a 401K as a substitute for a HiLux. Brides can be purchased for camels or cash. One is often easier than another to come across. The interest rate is adjustable based upon one's abilities as a camel breeder. I don't see very many baby camels, however. Maybe it is more difficult to breed them than one can assume.

The filthy children smile as we drive by and the giant dog barks defiantly while chasing us, returning to its post triumphantly as we drive past the camp. The Afghan dog shares the same basic traits as the American variety you would call an Afghan. Large, long hair, with a pronounced snout. The native version, however, is larger, scruffier, and a whole lot meaner. Each family compound has one, and they are very good guard dogs. I have one strict rule that no dog will be harmed unless it is about to rip a head off. The terps know the first thing to yell when I come into a mud hut complex is to "put the dog on a rope." If there is one way to turn the population against you it is to kill their dogs. At least that is true for Americans. I show some cultural arrogance and attribute that feeling to Afghans as well.

Dog fighting is a big "tradition" in Afghanistan according to legend, but I haven't seen or heard of an organized dog fight since I have been here. But then I had heard a lot of rumors about Afghanistan. The rampant homosexuality, the extreme Muslim piety, the bad food, and the worthless ANP. So far, most of these have been well hidden. The Islam practiced in even this most Pashtun of provinces has proven to be both personal and private. While every village has a nice mud hut mosque, the call to prayer rarely has but one or two older villagers moving to the mosque. It serves as much as a meeting place as anything else. I often can't tell the mosque from any other hut in the village and stumble into it unawares. No one freaks out. The terp simply tells me, "Sir, this is the mosque; we should probably leave." No angry chants, no dirty looks. But the simplicity of the truth doesn't make for good storytelling.

The homosexuality, or at least homosexual acts, I have never been witness to, though in Kandahar the cleaning guy came by walking a little gingerly on Saturday, the day after the Muslim sabbath. *Kuni* is the term for "catcher" in Afghanistan, usually translated as "bitch." But that is one of the only words that needs no translation here. Everybody knows what a kuni is after about three days in country. It's the universal epithet hurled by Afghan and American alike. Despite Afghanistan being a landlocked country, it has borrowed heavily from the navy in one area: the belief that "givin' ain't gay." Kunis, who are sodomized, are considered to be quasi-gay and womanly. However, the man doing the sodomizing is considered to be right as rain. Most Americans see both sides of the relationship as being pretty gay. A common story goes as such:

Terp: "What is 'the gay'?"

American: "A guy who takes it in the butt."

Terp, pointing to his fellow terp: "THAT MAN IS THE GAY!"

American: "How do you know?"

Terp: "I screwed him in the butt last night."

Of course, this is never firsthand. Friend of a friend. Guy in the other district. The circumstantial evidence of rampant homosexual acts is fairly strong. But thankfully, for me, there is no proof. And I am just fine with that ambiguity.

The bad food is a flat out lie. The food is delicious if suspicious. Eat it without thinking too much and you will be fine, with only an occasional bout of the Afghan diet plan.

As for the worthless ANP, today will be a good test. But I am optimistic.

After three-plus hours of driving, the day is warming up and the sun is now squarely in the sky, with no hope of lengthy shadows to protect me. At 6,500 feet of altitude, the temperature has already climbed into the nineties. The trickle of sweat running down my back protected by my bullet proof plate pools uncomfortably in my butt crack before seeping through my pants and into the canvas seat. *Nice.* Adding to the sweat is the fact that we have reached the pass and now must follow the heavily IED'd road. While IEDs were a negligible possibility previously, they are now an unavoidable possibility as we begin the climb into the Sur Ghar Mountains along the track of road known as the Dab Pass.

I have overflown this stretch of road in a Blackhawk while doing an aerial recon. The burned-out hulks of Rangers and HMMWVs stand in silent testimony to how perilous the road is. Fortunately, we are not going the full route, but diverting quickly to Shabazkehl to the north. As we begin the climb, the HMMWV engine whines as Moore floors the accelerator and the vehicle obligingly downshifts to move its many tons up the increasingly steep dirt trail.

There is a small ANA strongpoint overlooking the entrance to the pass. Surrounded by Hescos, the camp holds about thirty soldiers with no US mentorship. This camp was overrun recently, with no casualties suffered by either side. I suspect an arrangement has been made allowing the ANA to return with the tacit understanding that they won't interfere with the Taliban's activities. Well, that really doesn't change anything one way or the other. I certainly don't envy the isolated garrison serving as not much more than low-hanging fruit to be plucked as a Taliban victory whenever they need it. The lone tower is manned by a skinny Hazara who waves casually as we crawl by.

It's unclear from the map exactly when we should turn off the main road; here I must depend upon the ANP pathfinder leading the patrol. There should be only one turn. The town of Dab, which sits at the western entrance to the pass, is not much more than a family compound. The majority of the buildings are long abandoned and quickly disintegrating from lack of maintenance. The mud huts are quickly built, quickly repaired, and quickly eroded by the sun and seasonal rains. Many of the villages are more ruins than occupied buildings and Dab is no different. No one is out, even at this late hour, which is a bit unusual. But Dab itself is unusual. There are no orchards in view; neither wheat nor poppy is seen growing. How the town sustains itself, other than as a roadhouse for the pass, is a mystery to me. Maybe a subsidy by the Taliban to provide lodging and food for its travelers coming to and from Pakistan?

In two minutes, we are through the village of Dab and turning off the main road. If the turn is correct—and there is no reason it wouldn't be—Shabazkehl lies to my north about three kilometers away. The road, designed only for foot traffic and donkey carts, dives steeply at what seems an impossible angle. I brace myself against the dashboard while Moore downshifts the HMMWV and Dhakal hangs on.

"Whoa!" is nominated and seconded by both Moore and me.

At the bottom of the hill, the angle is reversed and climbs up at a slope of twenty-five degrees, if not more. The engine is in first gear and screaming. The HMMWV's gearing ensures that the effort is rewarded and we peak the climb, seeing only sky as we seesaw down the next slope. We repeat this roller coaster movement two more times, and the peaceful village of Shabazkehl, only 500 meters away, comes into view. The steepest hill is yet to come, with a very sharp turn on a narrow path over a gully at the bottom.

"I'm outta here!" I exclaim, and Moore stops the truck so that I can guide him across. After four hours of driving, the mission hasn't even begun. But at least I am going to be out of the IED magnet and moving on foot for a while. The ANP and other Americans follow my lead, and the dismounted American soldiers and Afghan police lead the way into Shabazkehl.

4

DISMOUNTED PATROL

1032.

As we enter the village, Siar comes along beside me. Whenever I get out of my HMMWV, the terp comes with me.

My radio, on my back and under my CamelBak, is still turned off.

"Siar, could you turn this on for me real quick?"

A turn of the knob and a few seconds for the radio to do its magic, and I run a quick radio check.

"Any station, Crazy 6, radio check."

"This is Dookie, Roger."

My attempts to tighten up radio procedures haven't been entirely successful. But, technically, mine weren't to standard either. My call sign is actually "Crazybear." According to my predecessor, this was the name of a not-so-famous Indian chief. *Whatever.* It sounds like a deranged Pooh bear. As retarded as my call sign is, it is easier to stay with it than change it and create chaos. I would love to change it, but there really isn't a good enough reason. As Crazybear is a bit awkward to say, during operations it usually gets shortened to Crazy. And I am Crazy 6. The numerical convention for the military predates the origins of military radio. The German military staff came up with the idea of selecting numbers to correspond to the various positions.

The "1" is the personnel officer, often known as the "adjutant." The "2" is the intelligence officer. The "3" is the operations officer, and usually the highest-ranking staff member. The "4" is the supply or logistics officer, the "5" is either the executive officer or deputy commander, and the "6" is the commander.

Finally, the highest-ranking NCO is by tradition the "7." Rob is Crazybear 7. Swampfox, the team I am with, lacks an officer in charge (OIC), so Geno is technically the Swampfox 7. The lack of formal staff and squads makes names an easier way to work, so Dhakal is Dookie,

Genovese is Geno, and everyone else is designated by their last names if they're doing well and their nicknames if they aren't. Having been raised in a military that demands perfect radio protocol, this bowing to common sense still rankles. But I have bigger problems today, so radio niceties must give way.

"Sir, what do you want me to do?" Siar asks.

"Get a vibe. Nobody has been to this village that I know of. I think it is untouched. Make sure these guys aren't Taliban, and be friendly."

"What is 'vibe,' Sir?"

"Oh, sorry. Vibe. Feelings. Are these guys pissed at us? Scared? Do they want us to go away? I don't want to piss them off if we don't have to."

"Sir, fuck them. They are all Taliban."

"Siar, you aren't helping."

"It is true, Sir, they are."

What can I do? Lecture an Afghan on what Afghans are? What is a Taliban? I know the technical definition: "students." No one in this village has gone to school. Enemies of Afghanistan? Hell, they are Afghanistan! Enemies of the Islamic Government of Afghanistan (IGoA)? I don't particularly like Karzai and his bunch. It is hard to blame the locals if they don't, either. IED planters or guys actively shooting at your folks? Almost assuredly not. People who aren't actively against the Taliban? OK, I'll buy that. But so what? The whole idea is to do something about that. Or, more to the point, help the ANP be an organization that can do something about that. Or is it just about payback for 9/11? The fact is, I am here because they are here. And they are here because we are here. My country chose a battlefield and both sides have accepted it. After all that effort, it would be a waste not to do something with it. Getting an Afghanistan that is pro-United States at the end of it all would be a bonus and the final exclamation of, "We win. You lose." *Good enough for now.*

"Sir, ANP want to know what they should do."

Great, now I have to tell the Afghan police how to interact with Afghan civilians. The only thing I've told them is we're going to the village to check it out and look around, but they are ramped up like they're on a combat mission. Are we letting slip that this is only a diversion? Have they been tipped off? Is it because they're new and not used to getting out and about? Not much to do about it now, but it bugs me a little.

"Tell them to mingle. Be friendly. Ask what they need. Did they bring any HA?"

HA. Humanitarian Assistance. Stuff to give to the population as part of the "winning hearts and minds" strategy. Food, blankets, cooking oil, prayer rugs, clothing. The stuff is cheap and easy to get. One of the only missions the ETTs seem to do is to hand out HA. But the ANA doesn't hand it out, the Americans do. *Great.* That's how we embolden the ANA and build the government of Afghanistan. Giving out goodies. My idea was to have the ANP give it out, so it would sort of seem like the government of Afghanistan was helping the people of Afghanistan. The only problem there is the ANP would keep the HA and sell it instead of giving it out. So then I tried to distribute it to the ANP the day of the mission, but the UAHs were packed with ammo and water and there wasn't enough room to put enough HA to make it worth the while. Since we are a mentor team, we don't have the large cargo trucks required to make it work. Occasionally the team tries to bring some out. But not today. The ANP have answered back they don't have any.

Ortiz, the navy corpsman, and Gregory have also dismounted and are walking with Fahim, the other terp. I wave them over.

"Stay off to the side, let the ANP take the lead on this," I instruct.

"No problem, Sir," answers Ortiz.

"How long we going to stay here?" Gregory asks. He isn't a big fan of "sir" all the time.

"Figure an hour. Nomad is just leaving Sha Joy now. It's gonna take them two hours to get to a blocking position to the north and an hour before the Taliban notice. So we leave in an hour, Taliban scatter, Apaches pin them, and we clean up. That's the plan."

"Noted," Gregory replies and we all chuckle. I always say "noted" when they whine about something and I don't care. It's more polite than "I don't give a fuck," but dismissive enough for them to realize nothing is going to change. So I guess I earned it this time. But that is the plan and it should work.

"Of course, Custer had a plan, too," I remind them. More chuckles. We spread out and start checking out Shabazkehl.

The village is unique in that it is built into the foothills of the mountains. Most villages stop at the base and are built on a fairly level piece of ground or gradual incline. Shabazkehl has the same mud huts but they are haphazardly strewn wherever a small piece of hilltop was level enough to put them, so there isn't the scope of unitary family compounds symmetrically built alongside older buildings. Rather, the compounds are more roughly joined with no single wall encompassing them. Despite this being a strict Pashtun area, a few women walk about without burkas. Within the smaller villages, the burka is dispensed with as everyone within the village is de facto family. Since our presence here is such a novelty, curiosity outweighs modesty and I actually get a realistic glimpse of a normal Pashtun village. The glimpse is fleeting, though, as curiosity is satisfied and the women retreat indoors.

As I have no reason to suspect Taliban, we will not be entering huts and compounds today. The police are being friendly and there are smiles all around. The Pashtun are generally without subterfuge when it comes to feelings. If they don't like you, you get the "hairy eye"—the frowning face of unfathomable fury. But here it's different. Maybe it's because the Taliban don't care about the village, so they know we don't either.

"Siar, ask Shah Khan to ask the villagers what they want."

Sometimes villagers will tell me they want nothing and ask for us to go away. This is generally because the Taliban are active and will hurt or kill people seen to be working with the ANP. The most commonly heard reply is, "If you aren't going to stay, then don't come." This reinforces what I have seen across Zabul. Even in this most Pashtun of provinces, they don't like the Taliban, but they have to deal with them. The penalty for not working with the government is less severe than the punishment for not working with the Taliban. So Taliban are favored by default. If the IGoA would provide protection, the Taliban would go away. But how do 1,200 police protect 10,000 villages?

I continue to walk along the main street of Shabazkehl and check things out. In many ways, it's the same as every other village: mud walls surrounding mud huts. The hand-pumped well is missing, however. Ninety-five percent of all villages in Afghanistan I have seen have a well with a pump that was installed in the nineties by the UN. Some of them don't work, as the wells have run dry, but they are very common. The hillside location and permanent stream running through the village combined with the village's isolation appears to have left them well-less. The braying of an occasional donkey is heard, as is the barking of a defensive dog. The street urchins are there, but in lesser numbers than normal—again, the sign of an unvisited location. Ordinarily, the children know to mob Americans to get candy and goodies. I suspect that Americans may have never visited this area. It's only three kilometers from one of the most critical choke points in the province. The narrowness of the roads and lack of tire tracks show no sign of any motorized visitor in quite some time. No Taliban motorcycle, white Corolla, or ANSF Ranger has been this way that I can tell.

Sergeant Han, my liaison from the ANP, is talking quite a bit with one of the locals. The gestures seem friendly and familiar. I watch the interaction and subdued body language that's so different from that of the Arabs I have seen. All of Afghanistan appears like the Arab world, only toned down. The language, the gestures, the practice of Islam. Certainly the infrastructure. Similar, but less angry, less forced. Is this the Persian influence? Or the unique aspect of centuries of isolation combined with bouts of intense international attention?

Han, the local kid, comes from a village about fifteen kilometers away. He works day-to-day with us at FOB Apache and desperately wants to learn enough English to become an interpreter. Although he is a senior sergeant in the ANP, he has no "juice," so he's treated like a regular patrolman. How he got promoted is a mystery, as are many aspects of the ANP promotion system. So far his English has improved to "Fucky, fucky Taliban," "Fucky, fucky NDS," and "Fucky, fucky ANA." It's enough for Rob and me.

He previously wore an Oakland Raiders hat as his daily headgear in uniform. As all mentorship starts with the basics, Rob instructed him to wear a police cap to present a more professional appearance. He never thought of it that way, but now he wears the right hat occasionally. Today the old Raiders hat is on, combined with a pair of cheap sunglasses. Despite the hat, with his vest of ammunition, rifle, and uniform, he presents a respectable figure, albeit a heavily armed one.

It's not just the Afghans. The Americans, too, want to wear what they shouldn't and try to grow beards. My first day in Zabul I stopped at Viper Base, where the junior lieutenant acting in command was sporting his newly sprouted beard and complete civilian attire. The two of us had a one-way discussion about that. Simple stuff, and once explained, they understand. Get the soldiers looking good and the cops will emulate the soldiers. The results have come together, and the dozen or so police walking through the village and pressing the flesh present an acceptable appearance. Certainly improved. The multicolored turbans are absent from all but the gunners, who use them to practical application as impromptu dust masks while driving. One wears the pakol hat (made famous by Ahmad Shah Massoud) and a direct descendent of Alexander the Great's Macedonian hoplites. More common in the north, it is an exception in Zabul.

The officer, if not Tajik, was probably recruited from a different province. He is not talking with locals, I notice. About half wear the issued body armor, with the same bullet-stopping insertable plates as my own. The other half wear locally manufactured vests and dispense with the extra twenty pounds of protection. They have the basic load of magazines, and their weapons, while slung, are accessible. The 75th Ranger Regiment, they are not. A reasonable police force for Afghanistan? Maybe. Just maybe.

As this is merely a patrol and not a search, we stay on the main (and only UAH-accessible) road. The vehicles crawl along, staying discreetly behind the police far enough to provide support if needed, but not so close as to be intimidating. The diversion from the Dab Pass road brought us to the highest and easternmost part of the town. The road has extended about 400 meters to the west so far, and back to the Surkhagan Valley. On the map, the trail should go another 600 meters and break out to the valley, at which point the Taliban should know what is going on. It is time for me to add another pot on the stove.

A well-executed operation is a bit like getting Thanksgiving dinner right. Everything takes a different amount of time to be where it needs to be at the decisive place and time. Understanding these various timelines and working backward from a culmination point makes it important to get the various parts going at different times. This meal started with the ISR overhead. Then we started our journey in the wee hours. Nomad, the team from the northern district of Sha Joy, has left and is slowly making its way to the table, following a different road but in much the same manner that I traversed, avoiding the main trails. But the main course of this smorgasbord is the Apaches. And like any other special dish, Apaches take some time to get ready. The Apache was described to me by the aviation battalion commander as an armored flying computer. It takes a while to boot. In thirty minutes or so, the Taliban are going to know our true intentions, at which time I'm going to need the Apaches ready to go. Coincidently, it takes about the same amount of time to get an Apache ready to fly. Since it takes a week or more to get a pre-planned mission, I have to cheat a bit to get this dish to the table.

"Imminent threat." Those are the magic words, the ingredient to bring out the flavor. What constitutes an imminent threat is thankfully ambiguous and left to the discretion of the senior ground commander, aka me. In most cases, this means I am in trouble and need help to get out. But I am looking for trouble. An arrangement has been made, and it's time to get the ball rolling.

I walk back to my HMMWV, take off my helmet, and grab the hand-held microphone for the SATCOM.

"Zabul Base, Crazybear 6, over." As this is communication with a lateral headquarters, I use my full, ridiculous title.

"Crazybear 6, Zabul Base. Go ahead, over."

"Zabul Base, ICOM traffic indicates an imminent threat on my element, requesting standby Apache support." Now this is a flat out lie. I have received nothing on the ICOM, but it's really the only way to justify the greater truth. The fact is, I do anticipate being in a fight with a roughly equal number of Taliban. But the only evidence I have is my plan, my experience, and my gut. Back to Custer again. The only way to have the Apaches and the advantage is to declare the threat. If I wanna make an omelet, I gotta break some eggs.

"Roger, over."

The guy who took the call isn't Greg Cannata, and I doubt whoever it is knows what's going on. The wheels are turning now. The Zabul Base TOC is co-located with an aviation cell; there the battle captain resides. The battle captain is the commander's representative, always present to make the instant decisions when they need to be made. They're usually junior captains awaiting their turn at command—the "bench" should a company commander be found not up to snuff. If I had a staff, I would fire at least one of my commanders immediately. Unfortunately, I have no staff, and hence no bench.

The guy who took the call is probably walking over, at a fast clip, to the aviation cell. The request for Apaches is going to be approved by one of these young captains. I can only hope the aviation lieutenant colonel has told them what to do.

As I wait for an answer, Dhakal asks, "Sir, are there really Taliban on the ICOM?"

"No, I lied to get the Apaches."

"OK." Dhakal is soldier enough to know when rules are meant to be broken.

Moore, trapped behind the driver's seat, asks, "How much longer in the town?"

"About a half hour. Depends on the Apaches and when they are ready. When they are ready, we will move out." *More cooking.*

"My butt is sore already."

"Sorry, it is going to be a long day. You wanna walk?"

"It ain't that sore!"

Not everyone is really an infantryman.

After a few minutes, Zabul comes back on.

"Crazybear 6, Aviation requests clarification on standby."

"Zabul Base, roger. I want birds warmed up, pilots in the seats. Anticipate wheels up in thirty to sixty minutes."

The Apaches have promised me sixty minutes overhead, with a ten-minute flight to Abdul Qadir Kalay. If they launch too soon, they'll leave before we get there and the Taliban can hide and then flee. If they launch too late, the Taliban will hit the hills and we can't do anything.

"Roger, wait, out." He is going to make sure this is what is going to happen.

Only a minute later he breaks in again, "Apaches will be ready in forty minutes, Zabul Base out."

OK, the biggest failure point appears to be cleared. As long as the pre-flight checks don't reveal any great deficiency or mechanical problem, I should get the birds. Now, as long as the Taliban don't break out in the next forty minutes, there really isn't anything to stop us and the plan. *Maybe I'm not Custer. At least not yet.*

My BFT screen flashes in the upper right corner indicating an unread message.

"Having fun?" Rob is giving me a hard time.

"Sorry I left you behind." I do feel a little guilty.

"No you aren't."

"A little." BFT is kept short. Makes the conversations more fun sometimes. Levity in brevity.

"Have fun storming the castle." Another of Rob's and my favorite quotes, stolen from the movie *The Princess Bride.*

"Wilco [Will comply]. Don't stay up."

"I will anyway."

"I know." Nobody sleeps when a patrol is out. Especially when that patrol is in the Surkhaghan Valley.

Nothing I can do for the next thirty minutes, so I crawl back out of the truck and start walking down the trail.

I meet up with Ortiz and Gregory.

"Anything?"

"Nope, pretty boring." Gregory replies.

"Boring I can handle right now. Apaches are warming up. We should be in the valley in a little while." Even though we're walking with seventy pounds on, none of us is breathing hard and we all seem comfortable with the load, heat, and altitude. The latter two stand at about ninety degrees and 7,000 feet, respectively. The trail is taking us down to the wheat fields, shielded from the main valley floor by a 1,000-foot-high hill running north and south. This is an isolated little piece of paradise.

Afghanistan doesn't have a water problem. It has a water distribution problem. Parallel to the trail is one of the wonders of Afghanistan, the *karez*—handcrafted aqueducts that make agriculture possible in this arid land. The aqueducts are constructed of rock, mud, and sticks. They carry water to the fields from the few accessible year-round streams and springs. One of the ways the Soviets denuded the countryside of people was by destroying their water distribution system, built through the centuries. This destroyed the agriculture and made the now unfertile desert uninhabitable.

While the hand tool symbol of the American farmer is the pitchfork, made famous by the *American Gothic* painting, in Afghanistan it's the shovel. The shovel serves as the valve system for the complex series of ditches, dams, and outlets. A spade full of earth placed here, and the water is cut off from one of the flooded fields. A shovel full removed there, and the next field is flooded with the essential water. The farmer is only as useful as his shovel, much as an infantryman is only as good as his rifle. The Taliban know that to disguise themselves as a farmer is only a matter of dropping an AK and picking up a shovel.

The karez drops down with me and provides a serene backdrop to a fairly panoramic view of this hidden part of Afghanistan. North of the fields lies a deserted part of Shabazkehl. Long neglected, the roofs have disappeared completely and the walls are eroding into what looks like a ragged set of teeth. The doors, long gone and probably reused somewhere else, still have their empty rectangular shells. The windows have also been removed. Each room would have had one or two of these—pieces of glass approximately four inches square. Enough to confirm the time of day, but hardly enough to provide a lot of light or a sense of space. Prison cells have larger windows.

I have been in rooms such as these many times but it is only now, in their advanced state of decay, that I really see them. It's usually hard to see inside of them—in the transition from the normally blinding sunshine to the dust-hazed darkness, I am dependent upon the single beam of light coming from my rifle—and even harder to get my bearings or understand the full floor plan. But with their roofs removed, I get a full-scale blueprint standing above them. The pitiful smallness of the rooms and three-foot-high inner doorways remind me of the difficulty of moving about while in body armor. In one corner, the mud walls still show the soot of the abandoned kitchen.

Past the expanded family compound, terraces show through fallow fields long abandoned. These are everywhere. It's unknown whether it's because of reduced population or poor soil, but in my experience abandoned acreage outnumbers tended fields by ten to one. Cutting a line across their shield from the rest of Zabul, a single motorcycle trail reaches to the peak of the foothill. If the Taliban aren't interested in Shabazkehl, they are certainly interested in the foothills to the west of it. And understanding the importance of high ground isn't lost on the Taliban. I hope that whatever hills they hold later today won't be enough to counter my Apaches, still preparing to launch.

I follow the trail, which follows the karez, which leads to green wheat fields surrounded by almond trees. Not enough to be called an orchard, but probably enough to augment the diet and provide shade in the heat of the day. A man who appears to be about fifty tends the fields with what may be his son and grandson. The arithmetic of Afghanistan, to borrow from Kipling, distorts the appearance. Most likely it is a father and two sons. They all carry shovels, the youngest one with a homemade handle worn smooth.

Each wears a *salwar kameez*. The salwar kameez is the only civilian dress I have seen the men wear here. The outfit is well suited to Afghanistan, loose and flowing, shielding the skin from the sun without being too hot. The vest is almost always included for men who have sprouted a beard. I have two pairs myself, one given by the Region South chief of police, a towering Hazara named Wadat. In this field, the youngest of the three wears the salwar kameez in a faded blue. The middle-aged man wears the same in brown, but his advanced age means his dress includes a gray vest. High fashion for Afghanistan even for working the fields in the middle of the day. The oldest of the three, the *baba*, wears the same vest but his salwar kameez is in heavily stained white.

The three farmers seem pleased and curious to see the ANP and Americans. The baba steps forward and speaks with Han and me. Siar is there. Pleasantries are exchanged.

"Salaam alaikum. Alaikum al salaam. Singe, jure, pechaitai. Manana Tasha-kur." Back and forth with smiles and the proper hand gestures.

The fact that I speak Pashto with a not-too-atrocious accent pleases and amuses the three who smile at me. But only the baba speaks after the pleasantries; the younger two stand back in deference and respect. Han takes the rest of the conversation, and Siar, knowing it to be local talk and unimportant, is polite enough not to translate. Suddenly Moore shouts from the truck.

"Sir, TACSAT."

"Moving."

I smile at the three and say, *"Da Cho Da'I Pa'aman,"* the traditional farewell for Pashtuns, before I walk off. It took me about two months to learn to say it right.

But suddenly the elder calls me back and Siar sees fit to translate.

Still smiling, he quickly rattles off something directly to Siar. Both Siar's and Han's faces turn serious.

"Sir, he says the route we are taking could have some IEDs on it. The Taliban were on it not long ago. Whether they just drove or planted bombs he doesn't know. But he thinks we should be careful."

I never get this kind of unsolicited help. Certainly not the first time meeting a villager this far away from Qalat. Why he does so I don't know. False info? Possible, but why? Does he see us as guests, and therefore looks to our protection to the next village as is traditional in Pashtunwali? Possible, but nobody else bothers. We were uninvited guests, as memory serves. Was it the fact that I mumbled a few words of Pashto, therefore unlike the Soviets he may remember? I don't know and it really doesn't matter. We will drive out on the road regardless, but I will put dismounts in front all the way to the valley instead of just driving. We don't have mine detectors and it would take too long to go back around the other way. We have to take this trail out if we want to hit Abdul Qadir Kalay within an hour.

"Tashakur." Thank you. And I smile and exchange a final handshake with my right hand placed over my heart as a punctuation to the traditional pleasantries.

The HMMWV is listing to starboard and when I open the door, its weight causes it to snap open quickly. I don't bother to sit down, but grab the mic off the cord dangling from the roof.

"Zabul Base, Crazybear 6, you have traffic, over?"

"Roger, Apaches are in standby, ready to launch. Requesting estimate of time to wheels up."

Time for some quick math. The dinner is going to start soon so I don't want to miss a dish.

The trail extends about another 1,000 meters until it breaks into the valley. That's fifteen minutes at an easy pace since it still goes downhill. Thanks to the baba's warning, I'm going to lead with dismounts and the vehicles will follow behind. At a minimum, the Apaches have one hour overhead. Forty minutes for us to get to Abdul Qadir Kalay, and an additional ten to Surkhagan. It takes roughly the same amount of time for the Taliban to drive to the town of Surkhagan as it does for the Apaches to fly from Qalat. Plus, they will have to get organized for another five minutes. So the Apaches can launch the minute we bust out of the valley. But to plan the dinner without thinking of my guests is rude. Let them dictate the time.

"Zabul Base, Crazybear 6, any movement on the Taliban at Abdul Qadir Kalay?"

"Crazybear 6, Zabul Base, negative."

"Roger, launch Apaches at movement of Taliban from Abdul Qadir Kalay. That should be in the next twenty minutes."

"Say again, over."

"Zabul Base, I want you to launch the Apaches when the ISR picks up movement out of Abdul Qadir Kalay by the Taliban. Don't wait for me, over."

"Roger, got it this time. Will notify you as well. Good hunting."

"Thanks, see you tonight. 6 out."

Well, as long as the Taliban are going to know where we are really going, it's time to tell the ANP.

"Siar!" I yell out.

He hustles over, asking, "What's up, Sir?"

"Grab Shah Khan and have him come over."

Siar talks into his police radio.

While I wait, I sweep the dust off the naan with my hand and munch on the quickly hardening bread while I crack open a water bottle. I have been on my feet for about an hour and walking. Not hard, but the heat takes a toll and under my body armor I am drenched in sweat. My face and arms are dry, not from lack of perspiration but from the near instantaneous evaporation in the dry climate. My CamelBak remains full;

I haven't touched it yet. It's for emergencies, when I really need it. The naan will be trash in another hour, then it's jerky and goo packets. *Enjoy it while I can.*

Shah Khan walks over, smiling. Mahmoud is next to him, not behind him. That speaks volumes. He isn't smiling. More a personality thing. To get things across, I should probably talk to Mahmoud. But Shah Khan has the rank and was introduced as the commander by Sarjang. Maintain the façade.

"Siar, ask them what they thought of the village." A faux pas there. I normally don't speak through the interpreter. I would never do that with Sarjang or Julani. It's not deliberately disrespectful; I really don't know Shah Khan and I do know Siar. I realize the mistake as Siar translates and I tell myself not to do it again.

After the exchange of Pashto, Siar sums up a three-minute conversation with, "He doesn't think they are Taliban."

Good enough.

"Shah Khan, we are going to Surkhagan. I have the planes overhead at Abdul Qadir Kalay and they see thirty Taliban. The Apache helicopters are going to meet us there. We must get there as fast as possible as soon as we walk out of the valley. But we must walk ahead of the trucks to look for IEDs until we are in the valley."

Siar, while smiling, translates. Shah Khan's smile grows and if Mahmoud is capable of a smile, I think I saw a glimmer of it. Shah Khan says, "OK," and starts walking to his men. I pull my cell phone out of my pocket and see I have a weak signal. Most likely, in five minutes the Taliban will know everything I told Shah Khan. What they won't know is that the Apaches can shoot without being shot at and that they will be there in fifteen minutes, not forty, as I implied to Shah Khan. That should be enough.

The ANP are visibly animated, already moving down the trail. One of the PKM gunners in the back of the truck straps on a helmet. Few of the ANP with me today have ever fought in Surkhagan, but they all know about it. Gregory walks a few meters behind me as I stride quickly to reach the lead bunch. No more deception. No more feints. Now it's a race to see if we can get there before the Taliban can run away.

I look back and see the three farmers still waiting to see us leave, not yet returning to their labors. I give a quick wave and they wave back, smiling. I turn my back not only to the three, but to the tranquility of Shabazkehl. I hope today will be a journey toward more tranquility for all of Zabul, but suspect it won't. This is a fight. This is payback. For maimed and murdered Afghan police, Americans, Romanians. A lot of people want to see the Surkhagan Taliban hit hard and I am one of them.

But mostly this is about me. For twenty years I have worn a uniform and maintained the self-image of a competent, professional warrior. Today will give lie to or forever prove the truth of that self-image. It's not supposed to be that way. But the one thing I've learned is that this war is never the way it should be. I doubt that any war is. And I am OK with that. I lengthen my stride to match the aggressive pace of the police and move down the trail to the Surkhagan Valley.

5

CHARGE!

1143.

The trail moves more down than up, with more turns than it appeared to have when I examined it on the map or looked down on it from Shabaz-kehl. My pace is the standard fifteen-minute mile that's used as the standard for most army schools. About as fast as I can comfortably walk with fifty pounds on my body. I have marched this pace many times in the past and fall into it easily. I suddenly realize that the idea of dismounting and walking to spot IEDs is silly. At this pace, people aren't noticing much of anything. *Oh, well.* Because the road is so small and poorly kept (if at all), we wouldn't be driving much faster, regardless. Besides, I would rather be out of the truck than in it if we hit an IED. My mind certainly isn't on IEDs; I am foolishly thinking ahead. *How long till the Taliban notice? How long till they flee? Will the Apaches get there in time? Will we get there in time?* Thoughts of casualties aren't included. The fight is secondary. Get there firstest with the mostest. Twenty-first century warfare meets biblical-era tribes and Civil War-era maxims.

Time is never neutral. It will always favor one side or the other. Before now, time was on my side. Up till now, I had all day, assuming the Taliban didn't catch on to what we are doing. Even if they did, we would have continued on for the presence patrol and saved the plan for another day—hopefully changed to correct the failings. But much as a chess timer can reverse the pressure of time, time has shifted firmly into the Talibans' favor. If I take too much time, they flee safely into the mountains and the essentially unguarded region of Naw Bahar to the east. Naw Bahar is a recent administrative addition to Zabul, formerly part of Ghazni Province. Ghazni is part of ISAF Regional Command East, and I have had zero interaction with the Polish forces providing the bulk of the combat power there. Ghazni, despite being part of the Highway 1 corridor, has no common border with Pakistan and is considered of secondary importance to those whose strategy is guided by PowerPoint and maps. A closer analysis would demonstrate that the border of Paktika and Zabul provides ample opportunity for the Taliban to operate freely in Ghazni, which, of course, they do. In fact, the Taliban I am hunting today have most likely come from Ghazni, where they use the district of Nowah to refit and train before coming into Zabul. The Naw Bahar/Nowah border is only a recent addition to the map and, in reality, doesn't exist. Certainly not to the Taliban. A maxim of war is to "split the seam": find a gap between two units and exploit the inevitable weakness created. Basing military boundaries on administrative and unnaturally straight lines is convenient but foolish. The entire country of Afghanistan suffers similarly. But it takes real knowledge of the area to avoid such mistakes, and the US Army is sorely lacking there. Maybe the Afghans could help us, but two questions hinder that option: Do they really want to help and risk self-sufficiency? Even if they tried, would we listen? I have guessed the answer to both those questions and come up in the negative.

My knowledge, learned through hours of listening to and probing Sarjang and Julani, informs me that if we miss them before they get into the hills of Surkhagan, they will flee to Ghazni and relative safety. These thoughts roll over and over in my head. They amplify the stress of time so that I'm physically moving faster, trying to hasten getting through this pass, into my truck, and then essentially in a full-blown mounted cavalry charge across the Zabul plains.

The tire tracks I follow show a mix of the ANP Rangers to my front and the unmistakable thin bands of the ubiquitous Yonda motorcycles, the Pakistani rip-off of the Honda brand. As long as those are there, I should be OK. I only have another 200 meters until I am past the protective foothills and into the open. Moving so quickly, I have grasped my M4 with one hand forward of the magazine well, allowing me to swing my arms naturally. I shift the rifle to my other hand and forgo any semblance of tactical preparedness. *Faster. Faster.* The ANP to my front somehow feel the same pressure and now we are all in a slight jog in the narrow pass.

At last the Surkhagan Valley spreads before me. Moore stops the truck without instruction and I quickly climb in. I throw on the headset so I can communicate with the crew. Instructing Moore to move out, I double-check the BFT screen. It's clear. Moore asks which way and I tell him to follow the ANP.

He asks, "Which group?"

What? I look around and realize it has all gone to hell already. I failed
to remember that the team I am with only promised to get me to Shabazkehl. Beyond Shabazkehl, they don't have the first clue how best to get to
Surkhagan. In fact, Swampfox and I have spent more time in this valley
than the ANP. I look around again and realize that two ANP trucks are
paralleling a trail that runs right along the base of the foothills. I know that
road all too well and have taken it. It is intersected by innumerable wadis
and slow as hell. Only three to five kilometers in front of us is another
trail I've taken that has good bypasses and lets us get there faster. At least
that's what I think.

What's worse, Swampfox's two trucks have broken off and are following the two ANP trucks. The three other ANP trucks are behind my
truck, which is now in the lead. Ordinarily, I would tell everyone to stop,
reconsolidate, and come up with the best way to go forward. But I can't.
We can't waste a minute and that would take at least ten. *Tick, tick, tick.*
Insubordination and lack of planning aside, we still need to get to Abdul
Qadir Kalay as fast as possible. The trail I am trying to get to goes straight
there and it is quick. The road that Swampfox is taking goes straight to
Surkhagan. I'm convinced that it would still be quicker to take my trail
to Abdul Qadir Kalay and then turn to Surkhagan. But I can't wait for
Swampfox to turn around, either.

Fuck it.

"Swampfox 7, Crazy 6."

"Go." Geno sounds excited.

"Why the hell did you break off with them?"

"I think it is faster." *Bullshit.* He wanted to get away from me so he
could do his own thing. If he was going to break off, he at least should
have told me. I will have to deal with that later.

"Whatever. Get to Surkhagan as fast as you can and then turn to Abdul
Qadir Kalay when you get there."

"Roger."

"I am going to hit the trail ahead and go straight to Abdul Qadir Kalay,
6 out."

Maybe they will get there faster. I have lost some combat power by
splitting the forces, but I should still have enough with the Apaches to
handle anything the Taliban can bring without Geno and Gregory. It's
a little bit of risk, but I should be able to handle it with the ANP. I have
fifteen ANP and three US, plus Siar. Against thirty Taliban. Fortunately,
they suck. I also find myself in the uncomfortable position of being the

lead truck. Out in the open this isn't an immediate problem. It will be a problem when we hit the trail, with its predictable choke points. Splitting the forces creates an instant reserve. Of course, I won't know who the reserve is until one unit makes contact and the other doesn't. Maybe I should have thought this out a little better. I wish Julani were here. This definitely wouldn't have happened with him. I feel sheepish for not thinking this through and angry that my sergeants took off without orders. But wouldn't I do the same in their shoes? Probably not. *Too bad, press on.*

"Moore, move straight on as fast as you can. When you get to the trail turn right."

"Roger."

"Sir, which way you want me to look?" Dhakal asks. With three HMMWVs, the sectors of fire are based upon which truck you are in the convoy. Lead truck looks ahead, rear truck looks to the rear, and the middle truck covers the higher-risk side while the weak side is covered by everyone else looking out the windows and the lead and rear gunners cheating a bit to the weak side. But now it is just my truck and that convention is out the window. In the absence of a good idea, I punt.

"Whichever way you think the Taliban are going to come at us."

"Roger."

No sooner did I clear that up than Moore slams on the brakes. The open stretch of desert stops abruptly at a steep wadi.

I manage to mumble a stream of profanity in near silence, untangle my headset cords, and get out of the truck. Looking around, I see a slightly less steep embankment off to the side. I get Moore to look at me and I guide him down carefully. It appears as though the wadi will take us to the trail as well, so I jump back in the truck as Moore accelerates and the ANP behind us lag as they negotiate the steep wall. Not 100 meters later the wadi inexplicably disappears and we are trapped in a ditch. This time the stream of profanity does come out in varied and creative ways. I haven't even had time to reconnect my headset wires as I step out again and search on foot for a way out of the wadi that I worked hard to get into. I find one, sort of. I am not sure the HMMWV can make it.

"Dhakal!" I shout. "Tell Moore to jam into four-low."

The extraordinary gearing of the HMMWV allows it to go up seemingly impossible slopes, and this one seems impossible. Moore takes a few seconds, which seem like an eternity, to downshift. He is finally ready, and the HMMWV lurches effortlessly up the forty-five-degree slope. I wait a moment while he shifts back into four-high to make sure the ANP make it. Each Ranger is hand pushed up the slope until the four vehicles are back up onto the Zabul plain.

My frustration, combined with the pressure of the ticking clock, is magnified when I look around and see Swampfox following the other two Rangers effortlessly and already two kilometers down the road to Surkhagan. I have gone about 400 meters in a perpendicular direction. I get back in the HMMWV and, without putting on the headset, tell Moore to move on. The BFT screen shows a flashing message reminder. Bumping along in the HMMWV, I awkwardly open the message and try to read it.

"TB leaving AQK. Two groups opposite directions. Apaches wheels up. Advise."

I could try to type out a message, but it is quicker to use SATCOM. I grab the hand mic and break in.

"Zabul Base, Crazybear 6, over."

"Zabul Base, go."

"Which group is bigger out of Abdul Qadir Kalay?"

"Eastern group, over."

"Roger, follow eastern group and hand off to Apaches, have ISR monitor western group after hand-off."

"Roger."

"Crazybear 6, out."

I didn't see that coming. Why the split? Local boys heading to their home villages while the Pakistanis and pros head to safety in the hills and Naw Bahar? Diversion? Commander goes with the smaller group and uses the larger group as bait? Possible, but that requires a prediction that we have the ISR and Apaches. It is possible he knows about the UAV overhead. They do make noise, though it is nearly impossible to hear. Not that it matters, but I figured they would stick together. I was about to check on Nomad's position to the north and figure out how to use them when Moore comes to a halt.

I look up to find myself on a desert peninsula flanked by two seemingly impassible drop-offs. Two wadis have converged. I spring out of the HMMWV, infuriated. The rage inside of me, combined with the pressure knowing that right now the Taliban are fleeing while I am trapped in this damned desert and the embarrassing fact that my two other HMMWVs are making steady progress because they made the right call and I didn't, causes something inside of me to snap.

Almost involuntarily, I rotate the selector switch on my rifle from "safe" to "semiautomatic" and fire three rounds into the walls of the wadi while yelling at the top of my lungs.

Dhakal yells, "Sir, where are they?" He assumes, reasonably, that I am shooting at Taliban.

I feel amazingly stupid. "Nowhere, I am just pissed off."

"You scared the shit out of me, Sir. Don't do that." He is right, of course. I shouldn't do that. Ever. Not that shooting the gun is bad, by itself, but I've lost control. These guys are looking at me to make the right decision, at the right time, to keep their ass alive and I just instantly, in a fit of rage, put that trust into question. *You idiot,* I think to myself.

But it worked. Dhakal's chastisement and the act of yelling has expelled the frustration and anger.

Maybe I'll catch them or maybe I won't. I'll do the best I can with what little I've got. If I don't catch them, the Apaches will, or maybe Geno and Gregory with their ANP. Or maybe no one will and this will all be a waste. But I realize that I can't squander my command authority on fits of impotent rage. It's a luxury I simply can't afford and it doesn't help one way or the other. I am quickly thankful I only looked like an idiot in front of these two and not the whole team.

I read once that Colin Powell had a saying: "Get mad and get over it." Anger is an emotion that comes easily to me. Obviously, too easily at times. But just as easily the anger dissipates. No slow, cold buildup ending in volcanic eruptions. Short fits of controllable anger come and go like waves on a beach. This wave of anger has passed quickly and with minimal damage.

In only seconds, I have transitioned to a relative state of calm and I get back to the task at hand: finding a way through the wadis we are in. That's my problem right now and it is the only problem I can fix. So I start to fix it. Looking around, I see where a ninety-percent bank appears closer to sixty. It's worth a try. Again catching Moore's eye, I guide him down the bank using hand and arm signals. The nose of the HMMWV digs into the dirt but not enough to slow the momentum, and the HMMWV grunts its way through in a cloud of dust with a slightly damaged hood. The higher-lifted Rangers clear the bank easily. Rather than getting back in I walk till finding the best way out of the wadi I've led us into. With an unrestricted view, I quickly find an easily traveled bank that the HMMWVs and Rangers effortlessly get up and over.

I climb back into the HMMWV and apologize to Moore and Dhakal. They don't feel a need to respond, and Moore moves westward again in search of a line on a map I'm starting to question even exists. Several more times the same deliberate guiding of my HMMWV is repeated. But I have calmed to the point where it isn't an issue. Swampfox is making good time. I can see their icons steadily progressing on my BFT display. Crawling closer to the towns on the map where I know the Taliban are moving. I still worry that my combat power is diluted and, if they get there without air support, I am assuming a lot of risk. More to the point, they are taking the risk.

After about fifteen minutes of this, I finally reach the main trail about ten kilometers away from Abdul Qadir Kalay. At the same time, the Apaches come across the net.

"Any Crazybear element, this is Repair 32, over." The caller's voice pronounces it "three-two."

Repair? That can't be right. An Apache unit is going to have a cool name like "Reaper" or "Death Merchant" or "Killer." Repair? *Must have heard that wrong.* Since 32 is a unique number and it isn't shared, I drop the first name and just go with the number rather than mess up their call sign on the net.

"Three-two, Crazybear 6, go." Gotta drop the "6" bomb on them. I am the dude in charge. *Not that they care.* It is more a reminder for Swampfox than anything else. Not that that is going to do any good, either.

I can see the Apaches high overhead, about 1,500 feet above the desert. With the ground-level elevation at 6,000 to 7,000 feet and the heat, the heavily laden Apaches are going to suffer a bit. No hovering today, that is for sure. As they go over Abdul Qadir Kalay, they have already picked up the Taliban motorcycles. They inform me they've found two motorcycles going from Abdul Qadir Kalay to a village north of Surkhagan. I check the BFT. On the map I can see the icons representing the Apaches move on the screen in real time, as the screen refreshes every ten seconds or so.

Then the ghost of Clausewitz and the legend of Murphy and his infamous law drop in unexpectedly, but certainly not surprisingly. I can hear the Apaches on the radio, but they can't hear me. Fortunately, Swampfox can hear me, but they have a hard time hearing the Apaches. So everything has to be repeated twice. It takes three minutes of what would be a funny comedy sketch in another situation before everyone figures out what is happening and what to do about it. So Geno will act as relay for me to the Apaches.

The motorcycle count is frustrating. My hard and fast rule is: more than two, it's Taliban. With weapons, it's Taliban regardless. If there are two guys on each bike, it's Taliban. So I ask over the net, "How many guys?" Geno relays and I hear that the Apaches can't tell yet. They should be able to tell soon. But I have to stop them now before they get in the hills.

"Put a shot right in front of them and get them to stop. Don't let them get in those freakin' hills. If they do, they are gone."

Geno doesn't relay the instructions as Repair 32 comes across with, "Roger." OK, radios are working again as they should for a second.

But then, for three minutes, I hear nothing on the net from the helicopters. Gregory tells me he is in Qadir Kalay and he is going straight for Surkhagan. His route should have taken him through Surkhagan to Qadir Kalay. I guess that he found a detour but I don't know for sure.

I kick myself again for not keeping the units together. They should have followed me on general principle. But the fact is they know Surkhagan better than I do. Still smarting over my loss of control earlier, I am not angry. Right now I am just frustrated. I've got the enemy by the balls. I've got the Apaches right where I need them but they aren't doing anything but flying around silently. Maybe they are talking on the radio, but not to me. Maybe they are just as frustrated talking to an unseen, unknown higher headquarters, begging for permission to fire. And since I, the senior ground commander, am not there to verify the target, they can't get the permission. My zen holds out, surprisingly. There is nothing I can do about it now.

"Roger, Swampfox 2. I am about ten minutes back unless I get caught somewhere along the way. Keep pushing," I reply.

"Roger."

Don't stop. Thirty Taliban for the picking? Wild horses couldn't hold them back now. At least they are aggressive. I can put up with a lot of ill discipline as long as they stay aggressive. *Better the reins than the spurs.*

Repair 32 suddenly breaks in: "We have guys with weapons on motorcycles. We are going to engage."

Hallelujah!

Then more silence. The HMMWV is traveling at breakneck speed straight down the dirt road. The three ANP Rangers are in a row behind me. God help us if there is an IED on the trail because I am guaranteed to eat it. Is the risk necessary? Probably not. Geno and Gregory are already heading there. Qadir Kalay is only a few klicks up. The blood is up, and both Moore and Dhakal want in on the fight. *Screw it. Roll on.*

Dhakal comes over the intercom, "Sir, the Apaches are firing!"

Hallelujah!

Within minutes we are in Qadir Kalay at the exact mud hut where all the motorcycles were parked. I pull over to let the ANP do a quick sweep of the village; just as well, as one of the ANP vehicles has a shredded tire that has to be changed. I step out of the HMMWV and listen to the radio. The sound of the 30mm cannon comes across the valley about every thirty seconds. Ten-round bursts to thirty-round bursts. *Music, sweet music.* I feel the smile spread across my face. I look up at Dhakal; he wears a grin as well. Three ANP are doing their Daytona 500 pit crew impersonation on the tire while the other fifteen or so cops check the scattered mud huts. I am quite content to listen to the thumping of the 30mm cannons across the valley floor and the confused radio chatter.

Half of the traffic is Geno and Gregory, wisely confirming that the Apaches know *exactly* where they are and asking for help to guide them onto the Taliban. The Taliban have been fairly predictable thus far. Aside from splitting up, which I didn't predict, they ignored the Apaches, thinking they were safe as long as they didn't antagonize the flying tanks. Once the Apaches opened up, the Taliban froze, hiding in the orchards under trees. With the modern thermal technology, it is much easier to see a moving target than a static one. The desert surface and the Taliban body temperature are about the same.

The Iraq-centric army lingo slips in as the Apaches relay locations using terms like "palm groves." We don't have palm groves in Afghanistan. We have orchards. I guess they all look the same at altitude and through the monochromatic forward-looking infrared radar (FLIR) display.

The guns run silent for a bit as the Apaches, I assume, look for targets.

Gregory cuts into the net, "Be advised there is a dismount in all black on the hill between the ruins and Surkhagan."

"Yeah, we have eyes on that dismount."

"That dismount walking looks like he is carrying hay."

Gregory replies, "Roger. Not dangerous enough to kill, I guess." A little disappointment is clear in his voice. I feel no reason to interrupt. My two young NCOs (non-commissioned officers) are doing just fine without any input from me.

"If you look over, you can see a motorcycle burning. That's where two guys are hiding. Be careful." I wonder who envies whom the most. The omnipotent gods of the sky circling overhead are impressive. But the army comes down to a guy on foot moving toward an enemy on foot. I can quickly acknowledge that today wouldn't happen without the Apaches, but I still wouldn't want to be them. Being on the ground is where I am happiest. Listening to my soldiers move to the fight unbidden is a satisfying feeling as a leader and fellow soldier. Twenty years of soldiering and it culminates in listening to a fight on a radio. As George Peppard would always say on *The A-Team*, "I love it when a plan comes together."

"Roger, the black smoke? We are heading that way now." Geno sounds interested but not quite excited.

Burning motorcycles sounds good. Hell, I could just listen on the radio all day and be happy. *Finally caught those bastards.* The guy with the hay makes me a little nervous, so I decide to make sure we don't get too drunk on blood lust.

"Three-two, this is 6. Remember we have civilians in the area."

There is no reply.

Geno relays that his driver thinks he is taking fire from the hills. The Apaches are out of position and can't see it. The Apaches are doing yeoman's work. While they search for targets, they are talking Swampfox right into the engagement area.

"There is a road twenty meters to your right. That will take you right to the engagement area and me," one of the birds breaks across the radio.

"See the black smoke? Go straight to the burning hulk. That will take you to them."

"Do you want us to take out the motorcycles?"

Geno answers, "If you don't see guys on them, leave them and we will collect them." Don't want to destroy what the ANP can sell later.

Gregory now comes on, "We got dismounts going straight up the mountain."

A woman's voice comes across, "Roger, engaging."

Geno again: "Police are engaging. Nice shot, three-two!"

Ortiz comes across now. "Tell ANP to cease fire!" That sounds bad. Now the traffic is the familiar confusion and yelling. Being out of the fight personally, I can sense things are getting out of control. Combat is chaos; I need to make sure I don't make it worse.

"Swampfox 1, Crazybear 6. SITREP, over."

Silence. I repeat the request but this time to any Swampfox element.

"SHUT UP!" is screamed over the radio. I start to fume, but take a few breaths to calm down.

A few seconds later, Geno comes over the net. "This is Swampfox 1. We have engaged dismounts. One Taliban down, still engaging." *OK, he sounds pretty busy.* Sustained machine-gun fire from PKMs, 240s, and AKs was clearly audible over the transmission. I guess my previous call came at a bad time.

The Apaches have been out of the loop for a little while. Time hack. I ask them how much longer they have to support me. "Thirty minutes," is the reply. *Plenty of time.*

The Apaches give a callout of Taliban dismounts.

"North or south of our forces?" I ask.

"To the north." The pilots' voices are calm in obvious contrast to the rushed and excited voices of the ground elements. Probably for good reason.

Ortiz again yells for the ANP to cease fire. I am developing a picture that Gregory and Geno didn't stay together. SOP for Swampfox is for each HMMWV to take a different side of a town when in a fight and try to kill the "squirters" or "pissers"—Taliban fleeing the battlefield. It is possible that Gregory's ANP are in a position to fire at the approaching Geno and his truck, (with Ortiz in it). Why Ortiz is on the net and not Geno, I can't figure out. Maybe one is dismounted.

Ortiz comes across having found another abandoned motorcycle. *Lots of Taliban about. Good hunting all around.*

The Apaches come across the net. The Taliban are all now crawling up the mountains trying to flee the sweeping ANP with Swampfox. Again, the Taliban are acting as predicted here. I knew once the Apaches opened up, the Taliban would freeze under the trees. It is an effective counter-tactic. But now the ANP and their mentors are going across the battle-field on foot, killing those who stayed. The Taliban are forced to make a decision. Flee and take their chances with the Apaches, or stay and take their chances with the police. The consensus appears to be to flee. The continued thumping of the 30mm cannon across the valley shows that while this may have been the best choice, it still wasn't very good.

The traffic comes back from Geno, Gregory, and Ortiz. They are sweeping both mounted and dismounted and finding abandoned bikes. I ask for their location. At this point I think it is outside of Surkhagan, but just barely. It is Ortiz who finally clues me in: orchards to the north. In the ruins. The ruins of Surkay Tangay.

Say again?

Surkay Tangay.

I grab my map and, after some brief searching, I see it. There are no orchards on the map, however, just ruins. Like Shabazkehl, in the mountains themselves as opposed to the foothills. No driving in this area. As the combat continues, the radio chatter devolves to old habits. Prior to my arrival, the team nicknames were used regularly on the net as opposed to "Swampfox" and numbers. What started earlier in the fight as "Swampfox 1" and "Swampfox 2" are now, more often than not, nicknames. "Machete" for Geno. "Boomer" for Gregory. "Doc" for Ortiz. The last is common throughout the military. Navy corpsmen are always Doc, an honorific hard earned and justifiably prized.

Surkay Tangay is only 1,500 meters north of Surkhagan, yet it has its own name. *Good.* Ruins I can handle. Civilians mixed with Taliban make it much harder.

The Apaches come across the net now, but again with a breakdown of radio procedures.

"Out of thirty," comes the cryptic transmission.

"Three-two, this is 6, say again."

"Roger, just letting my wingman know I am out of thirty-millimeter ammunition." *Hmmmm. This fight is coming to an end on the air side. What to do about it?*

As I formulate adjustments to the plan, Ortiz jumps on again: "We have an RPK." Ortiz is excited. He'll have some stories to tell when he gets back to the fleet.

A message on BFT comes across. The western group of Taliban have grounded their motorcycles to set up an ambush. The Romos (Romanians) and ANP out of checkpoint thirteen are working together.

I check with the Apaches if there are other assets in Lagman to help out. Nope. Out of seven Apaches, only two are operating. The price we pay for all the computerized stuff.

With the Apaches running low (or out of) their primary ammunition, their usefulness as an ISR asset remains. But there is still the western group to be dealt with on the way home. *Gotta leave something for them.*

"Three-two this is 6. As you RTB [return to base] Zabul has PID on motorcycles moving west [*whoops!*]—correction, east from Highway 1 to Surkhagan. Coordinate with Zabul Base to vector you."

"You want us to break station now?"

"How much time you have left?"

"Not much."

I pause. The ISR is nice. Their help in guiding us to the targets was essential. But are they going to get more kills there or here? The guns have run silent for the past few minutes. Maybe the Taliban have decided to hole up in the hills, where they are never chased. If they have stopped moving, the Apaches are going to have a tough time engaging. *Time to let 'em go.*

"Roger. Go ahead and break contact here and see if you can get a few more kills out west. If you get a kill, relay location and we will pick it up."

"Roger, three-two out."

With that, it is time for me to get into the fight. The ANP have remounted, and only I am left standing around in Abdul Qadir Kalay. It's five kilometers to Surkay Tangay over a trail I have taken before. A final look around before I get back into the HMMWV. Before my door is even shut, Moore has started driving to the thin black smoke column rising over the shimmering desert plain. He knows where to go without being told.

6

HIGH NOON

1230.

I put on my headset and verify I can hear Dhakal and Moore.

"What do you say we get into this fight?"

"About time, Sir." While I have been quite content hanging back and just enjoying the day's success, these two have been excluded from what has thus far been the best TIC in Swampfox memory. As new members of the team, they are anxious to be a bigger part of that. It is not as if we were doing anything of value back in Abdul Qadir Kalay. The deployment of the reserve is one of those artsy parts of battle. There is no cookie-cutter solution. It has to be a gut call. Deploy too early, and I lose my flexibility. Deploy too late, and I may miss the crucial moment of the battle. *Better to be late than early.* I am, in all likelihood, a little late to the party. I can't see there being much left to do by the time we get there other than pick up dead bodies and drive home. But there may be a few Taliban hiding in the hills and orchards that Swampfox, with only ten cops, can't find.

With Moore driving, I have a few minutes to figure out the best way into Surkay Tangay. The BFT's topographic map is functionally worthless at this level of detail, so I transition to the satellite imagery view. This is hit or miss and always a few years out of date—not a major issue, since Zabul is a few centuries out of date. It takes a few minutes for the data to load, so I grab my laminated map and start examining it.

The 1:100,000 scale isn't the best. But 1:50,000 would be too big so I work with what I have. The three-kilometer drive to Surkhagan should meet up with a trail that takes us to the west side of Surkay Tangay. Get out there, get the ANP on line, and then we can sweep across and try to find the guys holed up and hiding from the Apaches that are departing now.

"Moore, once you get through Surkhagan, the trail should bend north. Stick with that and it should take us where we want to go."

Up to Shabazkehl, the ANP were in the lead. Now the US are in the lead. It really is fair; we have the armored trucks and firepower that they lack. We also have a better picture of what is going on. This is probably the first time in Surkhagan for everybody in the ANP except for Mahmoud. I still haven't figured that guy out yet, but he just has the vibe of being a "plant" or a spy. Yeah, Shah Khan is in charge, but he doesn't have that command presence the way Mahmoud does. I didn't see Mahmoud in Abdul Qadir Kalay; he must be with Swampfox. *Good for them.* The radio traffic has died down in the absence of the Apaches. Either Swampfox isn't talking on the net or I am in a dead zone and can't hear them.

My HMMWV has reached Surkhagan, and the road disappears and becomes a wadi through the middle of town. Mature almond trees line the wadi.

"Watch the branches!" I warn Dhakal. During an earlier firefight here, there was a bit of humor. My vehicle was in the lead through the town, and one of the trees snagged the secondary M240 machine gun on the turret, ripping it off. As the designated (and only) dismount, I jumped out to retrieve it, and somebody fired a burst from an AK at me. We were by ourselves—no ANP, and the other Swampfox trucks were to the north and south of the town providing overwatch. Rather than sit in the middle of good ambush terrain, I threw the M240 into the back seat and ordered my driver (the now-relieved E7 who was the previous Swampfox 7) to "Get the hell out of here!" while everyone laughed and the gunner swung around trying in vain to find the source of the fire.

Moore is doing a more adept job at avoiding the branches while I notice the town is completely vacant of all people. Firefights are nothing new in Surkhagan. Whether the people are pro-Taliban or pro-IGoA is unknown. What is known is they are anti-firefights in their village. The Taliban commander has thankfully made the decision to use the ruins to the north as his escape route, allowing us to avoid unpleasantries in Surkhagan, where I had assumed earlier in the morning the decisive fight would be. That has certainly simplified the problem for me. Whether by accident or design, the enemy has made his own demise much simpler. *Never interrupt your enemy while he is making a mistake.* Had they holed up in Surkhagan proper, giving weapons release to the Apaches would have been a lot harder and probably would have devolved into house-to-house fighting. Nasty business all around. *Not our problem today, thank God.*

In two minutes, Moore has successfully gotten through the deserted wadi in Surkhagan, and we are only 1,500 meters away from Surkay Tangay. As we drive, however, I realize the road we are on is taking us not to the western edge of the ruins, but straight up to the edge of the hill and the middle of Surkay Tangay. This doesn't match my plan. I double-check the map and see that we will be between Swampfox to the west and the mountains to the east if we continue on the trail. This might work out. If Swampfox is pushing them, we might be able to hit the Taliban on the flank as they run to the mountains. A hasty ambush would be a nice finishing act. If we're too early, no problem; we just walk toward Swampfox making sure we fire flares to mark the front line trace. If we're too late, I'll just head for the mountains and do the best I can. The biggest risk is getting shot by the ANP. I've already heard requests for the ANP to cease fire twice over the net. That's manageable. I've seen them shoot. If they aim at me, their chances are only slightly better than if they don't.

I get on the net and let Swampfox know that we're going to be driving into the middle of their engagement area and that we're going to try and hit the Taliban as they flee. I repeat it to make sure, with a final admonishment to "keep the ANP under control."

"Roger."

The vehicles are going a good eighty kilometers an hour across the desert and are stretched out sufficiently to allow the dust to dissipate enough to see. Because I'm in the lead vehicle, this isn't a problem. In what seems like only moments, I am in the orchards and abandoned huts of what used to be the village of Surkay Tangay.

"All right, Moore, close enough. Get to a stop and let me out." I double-check the BFT one more time before getting out and I see a blinking indicator showing an awaiting message. The Apaches got their final kill and have a grid. I zoom out my BFT display and run the pen across the screen till I get a rough idea of where they are. Across the river from Spin Ghbarga. One IED or ambush a week comes out of that village. Picking up dead Taliban from that area makes total sense.

Nomad's commander, Maj. Devon Gray, is close by. I forward the message to him, telling him to get with the ANP and make the pickup. His ANP have had probably five killed and twice that many wounded from Spin Ghbarga in the past three months. It will be good for them to finally see a little payback. Without waiting for a response, I unplug my headset and grab a water bottle. I have no idea how long we're going to be out of the trucks, so I want to save my as-yet-untapped Camel-Bak. Once I start moving, the water disappears like nitromethane going through a top fuel dragster.

Siar comes up beside and slightly behind me. I yell to Dhakal, "Stay as close as you can and keep your eyes on the mountains to the east. I get in trouble, you better come get me!"

"OK, Sir, but after I kill them." He answers lightheartedly, but not jokingly. *I love my Gurkha.*

I give Moore a thumbs-up and move to the hills to the west to cover the weak spot. I have about ten ANP around me, spread out about every ten meters. A not-so-abandoned mud hut sits in the center of one of the orchards.

"Siar, tell the ANP to check out the hut, carefully!"

Siar relays in Pashto, and two ANP break off. Unlike the sprint out of Shabazkehl, the pace is deliberate and slow. Eyes dart in each direction, searching for anything out of the ordinary. *There are Taliban out here.* Because I have been listening to the chatter on the radio and know the success rate of FLIR in identifying people on the ground, I suspect a few Taliban may have holed up. The optics on the helicopters work great for movement. But when somebody stops moving, it is a lot tougher. Especially when the temperature is 100 degrees. The body ends up the same temp as its environment. During the winter or at night, the body glows clearly. But not now. So, like pheasant being hunted in heavy brush, we could be surrounded by Taliban and not know it.

I think back to the cocker spaniel I had when I was a kid. *That's what I need out here: a Taliban pointer. That would help.* My Labrador retriever back home is pretty stupid, but he would at least be good company out here. In the movie, Patton had a dog. Commanders aren't allowed the luxury of friendship. Rob is as close as it gets, and I do consider him a friend. But he is a sergeant first. My sergeant. As such that demands a relationship that is different, and in many ways deeper, than mere friendship. But a dog knows no such boundaries. I could see my Lab out bounding around in the middle of a firefight, being stupid. Sitting in the HMMWV just panting and drooling. Maybe too hot for him and the kids would miss him, I am sure. *Just as well, who wants to tell a seven-year-old their dog got shot in Afghanistan during a Taliban safari?*

AK fire is clearly heard about 300 meters in front of us and the pace slows, almost to a creep.

I come on the net and try to figure out who it is. "Any Swampfox, this is Crazy 6, is that your ANP shooting?"

"Roger, mine and Taliban," answers Gregory calmly. *Hmm. Well, move slowly and hope for the best. This might still work out.* We continue to move forward on line. The ANP flank me as best they can, snaking up the western side of the valley as the vehicles crawl along the wadi/valley floor covering the east and probable Taliban positions. Siar's ANP radio is a constant chatter in Pashto. I trust him to tell me if it is something important. We are about ten meters away from the comforting presence of Dhakal's .50-caliber machine gun. The wadi slowly bends to my left, taking us to the west. I see an uparmored HMMWV about 600 meters to my left. The contours of the terrain may have amplified the sounds of the previous gunfire, but right now it seems that, based upon the range, the shooting I heard must have come from the Taliban.

Along the ridge I see the ANP lined up, shooting sporadically. *Curious that the UAH isn't shooting as well.*

"Hey, who is that on the hill? You guys see us?" I ask, with no attempt at radio discipline.

"Oh, hey, watch out, Taliban are to your right, up that valley. I can't see them, but we took fire from there and the ANP are shooting at something." It is Geno.

"Who else is dismounted?"

"Ortiz and Gregory, to your north. They found some motorcycles and are checking out another valley."

"How many ANP are with them?"

"One or two, most are with me."

"Swampfox 2, this is Crazybear 6."

"This is 2, go."

"Can you guys see me?"

"Negative, where are you?"

"Downhill toward the east, about six hundred meters away from Geno, between them and the Taliban." I realize how badly I have screwed up as I say it.

"I can see Geno from where I am at. Found some motorcycles but I can't find any Taliban. I think they are closer to you."

Is this a good thing? My pulse is racing a little bit; looks like I haven't missed the fight, after all. If I were smarter, I would be more concerned than excited. The sustained, but light, fire from the ANP should keep the

Taliban from moving too rapidly, if at all. Maybe if we pick up the pace I can still capture some guys. A few prisoners would go nice with the bodies and round out the day.

Siar gets my attention; he is quite excited. While I've been chatting with the Americans and trying to figure out what the hell is going on, Siar has been doing the same thing with the ANP.

"Sir, the Taliban are right up this valley hiding; we need to get them!" he exclaims. I am reminded that, to the ANP, my voice is still that of a twenty-two-year-old who *hates* Taliban. *Well, no reason to keep him from having his day.* I cross over to the east side of the wadi. The foothills undulate with tiny valley after tiny valley. Consistent dun-colored waves, each hidden from the other by the terrain, all running parallel from east to west. An accurate replica of the terrain of the high desert in Dugway, Utah, where I have trained before. Even the altitude matches, at over 6,000 feet.

It is the middle of the day, and even with the slow pace, slightly shielded by the orchard's leaves, I am sweating constantly. The body armor fuses the combat shirt to my torso. The water bottle I took is in my back pocket, still untapped. I grab it and down the whole thing, throwing the empty bottle in the back of the HMMWV as I walk by. I can feel the lukewarm water filling my stomach and quickly going through my body. The wadi has a three-foot drop cut from the edge; I crawl up, hampered by my body armor and weapon. Siar waits for me as I get up and lean forward. There is a motorcycle trail up this little valley just to the south, where everyone thinks the Taliban are. The sporadic firing from the ANP is heard every few seconds. I figure the biggest risk now is probably from the ANP shooting me by accident.

Excited shouts in Pashto are heard coming from Siar's police radio. Or maybe they're from the Taliban scanner he also carries. If it's something I need to know about, he will tell me. My pace is now as fast as I can walk uphill. Which isn't that fast on the face of it. But combined with the walking we have already done and the energy dissipated by being super alert approaching Swampfox and the Taliban, I am already tired. The grade isn't too steep, but it is constant. Siar and I are breathing hard. Siar reassures me that the firing is just ANP. The AK fire is punctuated by bursts of PKM. No M240, .50-caliber, or Mark-19 are being fired from the Americans. Either the amazing eyes of the ANP are seeing targets my guys can't or they are just shooting as a display of Pashtun chest beating. Regardless, it should keep the Taliban from moving. Fixing them in the now dismounted fight. My heart rate—based upon years of exercise and training experience—hovers around 150 beats per minute. I can sustain this pace and effort for the next two to three hours if I have to, but that's it.

The surrounding hills and valleys magnify, distort, and hide the direction of the gunfire. It borders on impossible to determine who is shooting at whom and from where. I am thankful for the absence of the familiar and worrying buzz and snap of bullets close by. So either the Taliban can't see me—which is the idea—or they can and they are out of bullets, or they simply can't shoot for shit. Either way, we seem safe from at least Taliban fire for now. I hold my rifle one-handed, not at the ready. My right hand grasps the pistol grip while the sling takes most of the weight. My left swings freely, allowing me to maintain the pace. My trigger finger is stretched straight over the trigger guard while my thumb rests on the selector. I can bring the weapon up pretty quickly from this position. Looking around, I see no clearly visible terrain features that might hide Taliban from the lethal distance of 200 meters or less. I am assuming more risk, maybe even gambling a little bit, at this point.

Siar shouts something in Pashto. Clearly winded, his voice doesn't travel far. His breathing and mine is labored but steady. *Keep moving. Catch the bastards before they get out into the safety of the hills.*

More Pashto comes across the radio; the tone is excited and hurried.

"They're moving up, they're moving up, Sir. We gotta catch them, they are moving up," Siar translates for me.

I can't move any faster, I think to myself. While I am moving squarely along the motorcycle trail in violation of all tactical principles, Siar is to my left and behind. He is paying for his adherence to proper battle etiquette through greater exhaustion. His breathing is getting harder and faster, though I can barely notice because I am flirting with my own anaerobic threshold.

"I'm fucking dying!" he finally exclaims through panted breaths. "Damn! Hold on Sir, hold on. I show you where the motherfucker is." He halts and takes a knee, aiming his Chinese underfolding AK to my eleven o'clock. A large boulder, approximately twelve to fifteen feet high, shows prominently in the next valley, maybe 300 meters to my front.

Siar catches his breath. "You see these rocks?"

"Yeah," I reply softly. Not for some semblance of noise discipline, but simply for lack of more air to expel.

"Let me shoot some rounds." In the absence of a more effective means of marking the area, he will shoot at it. The exploding dirt and rock of the impacts will make the area clear to me.

"You see that?" He fires two rounds, controlled.

"Yeah," I reply. I can see where his rounds are hitting but can see no Taliban presence.

"Behind those rocks," he adds.

I take a knee and aim down my four-power ACOG scope. Scanning first, I see nothing that would indicate anything there but dirt and rock. I'll fire low and see if I can't get them to move out or maybe hit them with ricochet and rocks. A steady beat of one round fired every three seconds at any and all possible Taliban hiding spots. My breathing quickly slows down. *Breathe in, hold, shoot, breathe out. Breathe in, hold, breathe out.* I catch myself jerking the trigger. Not because I see a fleeing target, but because in my exhausted state I can't hold my breath that long. Since this is more suppression and a recon by fire, my breakdown of marksmanship fundamentals doesn't hamper the intent.

"He is not down, Sir. He was moving before," Siar tells me.

I am frustrated. I have no clue what he is talking about.

"I can't see him," I tell Siar.

I have a four-power scope and I can't see what this guy does with the naked eye. Not the first time. *And they tell me Afghans are blind. Whatever.*

As Siar and I shoot, gunfire joins in from behind us. The ANP probably see what we are shooting at and are helping out, more in spirit than in efficacy. Looking back, I see Dhakal and the HMMWV a few hundred meters behind us, in good position to also put fire on the rock that Siar is positive hides our Taliban prey.

"Dhakal, this is Crazybear, you see where we are shooting?" I ask over the radio.

"Negative," comes the reply.

More shouting is heard on Siar's radio.

"You see him?" Siar asks.

I don't see a damn thing. What the hell? Siar maintains a steady cadence of one round every two seconds while I prepare to mark the target for Dhakal's .50-cal.

"I'm going to put a three-round burst of tracer where I want you to put fire at, over," I say over the net.

"Roger," Dhakal answers. My coupled magazines hold one full of regular ammunition and one of tracer. I swap them and take aim. The shouting over the ANP radio is more urgent. I move the selector switch from the semiauto and completely over to the burst. Another retarded part of the army borrowed from the marines. In Vietnam, untrained draftees (and often well-trained professionals) would "rock and roll" quickly, expending all the ammunition in their magazines in a single, inaccurate, and largely wasted burst of fire. The improved version of the M16, the A2, designed by the marines, sought to eliminate this problem by removing the full automatic capability of the M16 and replacing it with a three-round burst. Sometimes, however, I want a full auto capability. To fire a three-round burst on a fully automatic weapon is not difficult with training. The M4 I carry borrows that fire mechanism from the M16A2, limiting how I can use the weapon. I would use a three-round burst regardless in this case, but it would be nice to have that suppressive capability. Special Forces' version of the M4 has the fully auto ability. *Good to be SF.*

The first round goes out with no successive two behind. Not a problem; the nature of the mechanism is such that when I switch from semiautomatic to burst, the first time I shoot isn't always three rounds. But the next burst should be three rounds.

I squeeze the trigger, and nothing. The trigger doesn't even move! I quickly move to slap the magazine in place and realize it has fallen out. I failed to properly seat the magazine fully on the forward bolt of the weapon. The thirty rounds crammed into the magazine have compressed the spring almost to its limit, and the ammunition pressing against the bolt didn't move enough for the catch to engage the magazine. Feeling stupid, I firmly press the magazine back into the well and pull on it to ensure it is fully in there. It is. I pull back the charging handle and settle again into marking targets for Dhakal.

Two three-round bursts spit out of the M4 and settle nicely around the target area. From directly behind, the tracers are impossible to see, but from the side they should be visible.

"Do you see tracer, over?" I ask over the radio. Siar is having a heated exchange in Pashto with an unknown ANP on the radio while firing his AK one-handed.

Dhakal has seen nothing. Siar is changing his magazine, and I put two more three-round bursts on the rock behind which Siar has assured me the enemy is lurking.

"Did you see tracer, over?" I ask again. I look back; from my vantage point, Dhakal should have a view of the boulder, but he says he doesn't. I don't know whether he doesn't understand or just can't see. But continued firing of tracer is obviously a waste.

Siar has stopped firing and looks over to me. "What are we going to do?" he asks.

Well the first thing I am going to do is make sure everybody knows exactly where we are. Getting shot at by Taliban I can handle; the ANP make me a little more nervous right now. If Dhakal can't see where I am shooting, I am going to make damn sure he can see where we *are* before doing anything else.

"I am at your three o'clock. Do you see me, over?" I ask clearly over the net.

"Roger, I see you." Dhakal answers.

"OK, I am going to move up this hill and provide overwatch," I inform him.

I have no desire to get close enough to the Taliban for them to be able to shoot at us with any semblance of accuracy. I want to get the high ground on them, find them, and shoot them from about 400 meters away. With a good rest and the optics on my M4, I can hit with certainty. I have hit from 600 meters away, but there was a little luck involved with that. Inside 200 meters, even the Taliban can hit me. *So, get the high ground and shoot down on the Taliban if they don't surrender. Easy day.*

I again start to feel the weighted tyranny of time. The Taliban know the ANP can't hit them from over the hill. They probably know where we are and can guess what I am thinking about doing. So if they're smart, they're going to make a dash for the hills and take their chance with the ANP firing haphazardly from about 400 to 800 meters away. So I have to have the high ground before they get away.

"OK," I end my transmission and start moving before Dhakal can reply.

Siar is anxious, whether from the threat of the Taliban or the threat of them getting away I'm not sure.

"They are still shooting at the motherfuckers," he needlessly informs me.

"I know, we'll get them," I assure him as I rise and pick up the pace again. If nothing else, the impotent target practice has slowed down my breathing and pulse. I grab my CamelBak hose and take a sip of water. *Gotta get moving.*

"We gotta take that guy, Sir, he is alive. I know for sure," Siar excitedly tells me.

How he knows is a mystery to me, but I have to trust him. Even if he's wrong, he's certainly making the day more interesting.

As we move along, the motorcycle trail curves slowly to the north and directly to the rock. It appeared as though I would be able to follow it to the high ground to the east. The terrain has become steeper and the trail has adjusted to the limits of donkey, motorcycle, and me. If my intent is overwatch, I should swing east and off the trail, but instead, and without good reason, I stay on the trail and move directly to the suspected Taliban position. It is considered what is called a "natural line of drift." The most natural path to take. And, as I have been trained, it is the one I should never take. But I find myself taking it because it is the quickest path to the enemy. The clock is ticking yet again. I still have to get into this fight in a productive, personal way. Sure, I have fired some rounds, but at what? Siar seems to know, but I don't, and that isn't good enough.

My pace has slowed; both hands have taken firm grasp of my weapon. Despite my rush, I get more careful as we close with what might be the Taliban position. The slope evens out as the trail turns east and even goes downhill a bit. I am cutting right across the fields of fire of the ANP and Dhakal. Farther back I see one of Swampfox's trucks. I don't know whose it is, probably Geno's. I get on the net to make sure Dhakal knows *exactly* where we are.

We move on, one eye on the high ground to the east, another on the area above the boulder, which has disappeared from view as we dropped down the trail. I do a quick assessment of the situation and realize that what began as an attempt at simple overwatch on the high ground has now become a movement toward the enemy. Something is missing, however. ANP.

"Tell those ANP to get the fuck up here," I calmly order Siar.

"What?" Siar asks.

"Tell those ANP to get the fuck up here," I repeat.

"They should come over here?" Siar clarifies.

"I would like to have a police or two," I embellish. No reason to be greedy, but a few more would make me feel more comfortable.

Ignoring the radio, Siar shouts in Pashto, and his call is immediately answered by a burst of AK fire to our front, coinciding with the unmistakable buzz and snap of rounds flying near us.

"DAMN! What the fuck!" Siar shouts out. We both crouch down. Every sense, especially hearing, is now attuned specifically to identify the threat. We both swivel involuntarily as our weapons are brought to the shoulder. No threat is identified or found, but it is obviously there. *Time to find some cover.* I duck behind a nearby rock, just large enough to lie behind and point my weapon to the high ground on our east. The source of the fire is hopefully masked by the rock for now.

"You cover that way, I'll cover this way," I order Siar, indicating that he should focus his attention to our back and down the hill to our previous position. Achieving 360 degrees of coverage is hard with just two people, but it is the best option I have right now. There is nothing to return fire to right now that I can see. If they shoot again, then I can reassess that determination. Right now, I have a bigger priority.

"Tell those ANP to GET THE FUCK UP HERE!" I yell.

How yelling at Siar is going to help, I don't know. But yelling seems like a good idea as I realize we are 500 meters away from the ANP, who are supposed to be fighting, and less than 200 meters away from whoever shot at us. Siar yells again, but this time into his radio. Dhakal has seen the two of us drop down and heard the fire and contacts me on the radio.

"Crazybear, this is Dookie, over." Call sign protocol again surrenders to the urgency of the moment.

"Dookie, go." I surrender as well. *Screw it.*

"What happened?" he asks.

"I don't know. Something engaged on us from about two hundred meters away. I have no eyes on. You use your fingers, you use your fucking foot, you use your goddamn butt stroke. But you get those ANP off that hill and onto this one. We are moving forward, over." The butt stroke is a bayonet fighting technique that could be used as a nondoctrinal, but effective, motivational technique on slow-moving ANP.

Siar continues his heated conversation over the police radio. Dhakal confirms my instructions and asks again what happened. From his vantage point and the distortion of sound it looked like we got shot.

"We were moving to a good overwatch and then somebody shot at us. I don't know if it was ANP or what, but it came from the wrong direction," I explain.

Siar has dispensed with the radio and is now shouting directly. I join him.

"Come on, you motherfuckers!" I shout. Clearly, they don't understand the words, but my tone and intent are unmistakable as I wave them toward us.

Movement in my direction isn't to be seen.

"Fucking ANP," I mention casually. Fear to casual annoyance in thirty seconds.

A burst of traffic on Siar's radio, and he explodes.

"Damn, what the fuck? They are just looking for goddamned motor-cycles!" he exclaims, finishing with, "Son of a bitches." The grammar isn't quite correct, but the emotion is certainly heartfelt.

OK, think fast. Time to get the ball rolling.

"OK, get on the radio, tell them if they don't get their asses up here, we keep all the motorcycles."

While Siar gets that word out to the ANP, I tell Dhakal what is going on. I may need him to start shooting motorcycles to make the point.

After a few moments and no discernable movement, I decide to up the ante. If the Taliban are scarier than the threat of no motorcycles, I know something scarier than Taliban.

Julani.

"Tell them if they don't get up here I will tell Julani that they were fucking cowards in combat and would not help the Americans. I will fucking tell Julani that." I have seen Julani nearly beat a policeman to death for failing to show proper respect. Sarjang and Julani committed a bit of an etiquette faux pas by not joining me, despite my direct request. I rarely make direct requests of them, so when I do, they make it a point to try to fulfill them.

Siar puts that out on the radio and finishes with an exasperated, "Damn!" I chuckle at his final point. Interesting to note that his English has progressed to where he curses more naturally in English than in Dari or Pashto. I also realize I don't know a single curse word in either language. I make a mental note to learn some for just such a moment. Truly a failure for any combat advisor worthy of the title. Whether Siar used my threat or thought of his own, I am not sure. Regardless, the ANP can be seen running toward us now. Now we have to wait. It will take several minutes for them to get up here. If the Taliban dash now, so be it. I don't think they will, though. The menace of Dhakal and his .50-cal are probably scarier than anything I might bring.

"It is still recording," Siar informs me. I wonder what he is talking about. *Does his radio have a record feature?*

"I don't think we get anything from up there," I say, indicating the hills to the east.

"The shots came from my eleven o'clock." To the north, in the direction we were walking. My anger again has subsided from the ANP being, well, Pashtun. The myth of the Afghan warrior. The reality of the Afghan bandit. Sure, they will fight, if there is profit potential. But with motorcycles in hand, profit is achieved. Nothing to be gained by crawling up that hill. Man could get killed up there! *Fine, you don't want to take your chances with the Taliban? Take it up with Julani. I won't beat you nearly to death, but Julani will.*

The initial sprint of the ANP has slowed to a steady walk but still in my direction. *Good enough.*

Dhakal comes across the net, again asking who is with me.

"Right now it is just me and Siar," I tell him. *Nice job, moron,* I silently berate myself. At the infantry school in Fort Benning, Georgia, there is a famous statue called "Iron Mike"—the inevitable nickname of all such statues—showing an individual fighting man. On the plaque on the monument's base are the words "FOLLOW ME!" The motto of the infantry. The statue depicts a fighting man with a rifle in one hand and his free arm sweeping overhead in the universally recognized hand sign of "follow me." What the statue doesn't depict, and what no school teaches formally, is that after leading from the front you look behind you to make sure people are indeed following. This is not a given, as the past few minutes have clearly demonstrated. Especially with a bunch of ANP who don't speak my language and probably have never been in a firefight or ever trained in infantry tactics. Hell, I didn't even say "Follow me!" down in the wadi floor when I first started walking up this hill. I just moved silently toward the enemy and assumed they would follow me. I really can't blame them, though initially I did. I am forced to blame myself for not making clear what I wanted. At least I got around to it eventually and before it became tragic. At worst, the time delay means a couple Taliban live to fight again. Or disappear in the Pakistan mountains never to reappear. Another lesson learned today. I won't need to write it down; this one I won't ever forget.

Since I have some time to kill waiting for the police, I spitball with Siar about where to go. I still have the almost instinctual desire to climb onto the highest hill, now to my southeast. No matter what, high ground gives me options. It is infinitely easier to maneuver downhill than up. My vision is better. If I'm getting shot at, I can easily slip to the other side of the hill, invulnerable to direct fire. Options. Once up there, I can slip behind the Taliban and trap them between Dhakal's .50-caliber and my small arms.

"Siar, we could go up this valley, this one here, and then come around that way," I offer. Thirty-eight-year old US Army major to twenty-two-year-old terp. The idea of a direct assault is repugnant to me if I can avoid it. Unfortunately, the ANP have a much better understanding of the current situation than I do. Which means that Siar, having listened to all the Afghan radio traffic, knows the situation better than I do, too.

He thinks little of my proposal. "We are not going to find anything over there. All the motorcycles and all the Taliban are that way," he tells me. It is unquestionably my decision, and he is very respectful. But his tone is clear: *If you want Taliban, listen to me.* I did my own thing once already today and got to the fight twenty minutes after everybody else. Today is a success already. I realize it is time to bury my ego and listen to the twenty-two-year-old. Plus, he is probably as tired as I am. My idea involves climbing straight up a very steep hill in the middle of the day. I suspect he may fear the walk more than the Taliban. It is not an entirely irrational concept.

"OK." I don't really want to climb that damn hill, either. "Fatigue makes cowards of us all," Patton famously remarked. Well, in this case, rather than trying to get behind the enemy we are going to go straight at them. But Gen. Robert E. Lee said, "I was too weak to defend, so I attacked." There has to be a quote in the history of warfare to match the situation I find myself in, but an exact match escapes me.

In the background, an unseen bird chirps in alarm. As well he might. A nice breeze blows that was absent in the floor of the wadi. The dry air combines with the breeze to evaporate what sweat is exposed. My face cools but not much else.

Sergeant Dhakal is still a bit concerned about our situation and he comes across the net again, asking for status. A mother hen to his wayward major chick. His Gurkha blood must be boiling at being trapped in a HMMWV. He should be a dismount, but we just don't have enough soldiers. I never have enough soldiers. He tells me the ANP have started up the hill, and I confirm visually.

"Yeah, they are moving as slow as fuck, but they are getting up here." They are only about 200 meters away. I am not going to give them a chance to catch their breath. My punishment will be moving out immediately and making them keep up. I have no pretenses they will lead from the front; that is still informally my job. I am getting paid accordingly. *My plan, my day, my risk.*

Siar and I chat amiably and relaxed about the deficiencies of the ANP and the uncouth habits of the Taliban. Various vulgarities are exchanged as required. As curry is to Indian cuisine, cursing is to the language of soldiers. Embarrassingly enough, I am a linguistic chef of some note in this regard. When I returned from Bosnia many years ago, my new bride was patient with the verbal entrees laid before her for about a month. And then, after one too many casually uttered, "Pass the fucking salt," she said, "ENOUGH!" So somehow, I've managed not to curse around my now much-expanded family. But the minute the uniform goes on, it's like donning an apron. Wearing that apron constantly for a year has made the situation worse. I hope I can detox on my way home.

At last four ANP join us, panting in their uncomfortable mix of cheap wool and cheaper polyester uniforms. None wear the issued hats. Two wear plain Kandahari beanies, one wears a turban, and one is bareheaded. Three sport magnificent beards and are clearly Pashtun. The turbaned one has a PKM, the two older men have what appear to be Russian AKs with wooden stocks. One is too young to be determined by beard; I take him to be about sixteen. He has the AMD-65. He is clearly excited to be up here. I hope he doesn't shoot me by accident.

Wordlessly, I get up and start moving north toward the sound of the fire from the unseen shooters. They have learned enough in this brief bout of mentorship to follow me without being told, but not too closely.

My weapon is now at the high ready, and I'm moving much as an upland bird hunter moves. My steps are deliberate. There is no rush at this point. If they wanted to escape, they would have. If they are intent upon holing up, they shall. *Be deliberate, be careful.* The chess timer has been switched over again and now the pressure is on the Taliban—or at least it is off me.

Generally, the Taliban aren't chased into the mountains. There is an understanding. Take our motorcycles, but leave us alone. *Not today.* Whether the Taliban know the deal is off or not is yet to be discovered. The burst of gunfire that thankfully stopped Siar and me may have only been a quasi-friendly reminder of the tacit understanding up till now of the arrangements.

Banditry, not war, has been the way of the Pashtun hills and mountains for two thousand years. Americans just don't get it. We don't do subtle. If there are guns, it is war. You want something else? You need to drop the guns first. The Pashtun are subtler. Guns are a decoration to be wielded in times of peace or times of war and certainly during the more common mixture of both that permeates Pashtunistan. Whether the American monochromatic clarity helps or hurts our cause is a discussion for another time, at a much higher pay grade.

I am again walking uphill, coming to the peak of the rise separating my little wadi from the boulder, which is now in view again. It is a good place to hide, and I carefully eye it as we approach. Siar has moved closer to me while the ANP have distanced themselves. I know whom I can count on. But the back side of the boulder, perched halfway up the far side of the little valley, is unoccupied, as far as I can tell. I reach the top of the hill and can now look down into the rock- and boulder-strewn stream bed that has carved out this valley. I am about thirty-five meters away from the floor of the creek bed. I decide to stay on this high side and handrail the creek from the high ground. No sense giving up the hard-earned height advantage unless we have to. Besides, the trail I should be avoiding but that I've taken the whole way is going the same way.

Targets up.

Two figures dart out from a boulder in the creek bed directly below us. I mount my rifle and disengage the safety to the semiautomatic position. The target is running, the magnification of the ACOG is automatically going in and out as my brain processes the red chevron of the reticle with one eye and the running target with the other. My first round is behind; I have failed to calculate for the moving target. I swing ahead as I have done when shooting skeet, and my second round lands errantly in front of the target. I have the target bracketed and now have the requisite speed and lead required to hit the target. I can hear nothing. I stand square to the target, leaning in slightly, my body hunched over the M4 pulled squarely into my shoulder. The target has stopped; his hands move upward as I squeeze the trigger. The red chevron is apexed at the center of his chest and the target is down. I swing my upper body with the M4 attached to the next target, who is stationary with his hands up. My finger lightens on the trigger. As my auditory capabilities return, a dull snap barks out from Siar's AK. Second target down.

This has all happened in about one and a half seconds.

"Siar! What the fuck!" In those one and a half seconds time has slowed to an amazing degree, where each aspect seemingly took minutes. What was clearly a surrendering man to me could have been anything to Siar. Siar is confused.

"Sir?"

"He was surrendering!" I exclaim, but not screaming as I felt I should.

According to the American way of war, prisoners don't get shot. I am suddenly fuming at Siar. That we can transition from mortal enemy to protector in a split second is one of those aspects of American military culture so confusing to Pashtuns. Sure, they can do it for money or for gain. But just because a guy puts his hands up, we are supposed to protect them? The Afghans chuckle at the concept.

"Sir, fuck him. He was Taliban." I look down and wonder how he knows. No weapons, no ammunition vests, no military-style jackets. The only thing that would differentiate them from civilians is the lack of head-gear. In the absence of proof, it appears we just shot two unarmed men who were trying to surrender. I feel gut punched and drained. No massive rush of adrenaline, unlike my first few firefights. Certainly not the way it is supposed to go. I look down and neither of the targets moves an inch. Completely static. *Nothing I can do about it now. Fuck it. Keep moving.*

"We will come back for them later. Keep pushing up the creek bed," I tell Siar, who doesn't translate for the ANP.

While I feel deflated and question my decision-making, the ANP are animated and literally run past me, taking the lead and moving up the valley at an amazing speed. I am laboring to keep up. While shooting unarmed Taliban has left me with a sickening feeling in my stomach, the ANP see this as great sport. The pace is frantic and I tell Siar to tell them to slow down. He shouts at them and they shout back. Another target appears 200 meters up the valley with the ANP about fifty meters in front of me. This man's hands are up as high as he can stretch them. He has discovered that hiding won't work today. In one hand is a PKM held by the carrying handle. Neither hand is remotely close to the trigger. He is making no pretenses and no attempts at subterfuge. "I am Taliban, I am surrendering," he says clearly but wordlessly. The ANP, naturally, all shoot at him simultaneously.

"CEASE FIRE! CEASE FIRE!" I finally scream. Siar translates for me unbidden and the ANP miraculously do stop firing. They have each probably fired five to ten rounds at the guy, who has emerged amazingly unscathed. *Thank God for lack of training.* I am now running to catch the ANP, who are closing with the man who remains with his hands up, PKM still held high. Whoever shot at me earlier, it wasn't him. The PKM's sound is very different from an AK's, though the mechanisms are nearly identical. Probably the two dead guys I left back behind me. The ANP reach the Taliban before I do and start beating him with their weapons, the aforementioned buttstroke being the technique of choice.

"STOP IT, GODDAMN IT!" I yell again. *What the fuck is wrong with these people?* The ANP with the PKM has broken the stock of his weapon on the Taliban so he has grabbed the Taliban's PKM and commenced beating him with his own weapon. I finally reach the cluster of Afghans and the ANP are about to shoot the surrendering Taliban, who is still standing, though hobbled. One of the cops with the Kandahari beanies is leveling his AK on the Taliban. I grab the barrel of his weapon and shove it away. The other ANP with the Kandahari hat points his Russian AK at me as I stand between him and the Taliban prisoner. I still hold my M4 with one hand and stare into his very black eyes. The anger I feel is reflected there. I am daring him with my glare. Staring him down as I would a disobedient dog.

You gonna fucking shoot me? Because you are going to have to before I let you kill this guy, I transmit wordlessly through my eyes. I am angrier at the ANP than I am at the Taliban at this point. I expect this from Taliban. I know for a fact that if they captured me on the battlefield, I would be raped, tortured, and then have my head cut off on YouTube. But that is not how Americans do it. *And as long as Americans buy your equipment, buy your fuel, pay your salaries, and give you everything you have, you are going to fucking do it our way. MY WAY.* How long this silent stare-down goes on, I have no idea. While my eyes never waiver from his, I know his weapon is on fire, his finger resting taut on the trigger. It is pointed at the lowest point of my SAPI plate. If he pulls the trigger, it may miss the plate and hit my lower abdomen. I don't know for sure and I dare not look down.

Without breaking eye contact, I order Siar, "Tell the young kid and the guy with the turban to take this guy back to my HMMWV."

Siar speaks calmly and deeply in Pashto. The guy I am staring at lowers his weapon and smiles at me. I don't smile back. Siar takes the handcuffs he keeps on his pistol holster and handcuffs the Taliban prisoner who, I now notice, sports a surprisingly bloodless bullet wound in his thigh. Realizing that he isn't going to die, he collapses from the extent of his injuries. In only a short time, he has been shot and has taken a hell of a beating. The ANP will have none of it, however. They yank him up painfully by his arms and get him walking down the hill, bullet wound and all. I feel no pity for him. I almost took a bullet for the asshole. He is lucky to be breathing, much less walking. I realize that Gregory, Geno, and Dhakal are all trying to get in touch with me on the radio. I haven't said anything since all the firing began and Siar and I shot two unarmed men trying to surrender.

"Roger, been busy. We dropped two guys and captured a third. Dhakal, make sure he gets there alive. ANP tried to shoot him. Send more ANP up here and have them bring two body bags. In the creek bed they will find two guys. Just drop the bags near the bodies and we will get them on the way back. There are Taliban all over the fucking place and we aren't done yet."

"Fucking hooah, Sir," Gregory puts over the net. *Yeah, sure, I guess it sounds hooah when I put it like that.* But right now, I am not feeling hooah. Just tired, angry, and frustrated and I still have more hills to climb. I am left with four people, counting myself. The two guys with me are still seething with anger as I lead them slowly up the creek bed. I should be able to handle what Taliban remnants occupy the hills. I hope the Taliban have seen that if they surrender they will live, but if I find them they die. That should encourage them to be a bit more manageable. I am more concerned about the two ANP behind me. They could shoot Siar and me, blame it on the Taliban, and no one would be the wiser. *Hell of a spot to be in.*

"All right Siar, let's move," I order. We all fan out in a fire team wedge, Siar again on my left and slightly behind, the ANP on the far wings. I am, yet again, in the lead. Slowly picking my way up the creek bed, I again move with my M4 at the high ready. I start mentally running through my list of things to do and realize my weapon is still loaded with the same coupled magazines that I started the day with. I have fired enough bullets to justify a fresh one. I have no pouch to hold the coupled magazines, so I throw the half-loaded ones into the cargo pocket on my left leg and insert a fresh single magazine—ball only, no tracer. I pull on the magazine to ensure it is seated properly before moving forward again. I quickly become annoyed as the coupled magazines in my pocket bounce and chafe against my leg. *No more coupled magazines for me after today.* Since I am still waiting on the additional ANP to show up, I move slowly, sipping on my quickly draining CamelBak. The ANP and Siar stop occasionally to sip water from the creek. The trail I had been following has disappeared, and we snake around the rock-strewn creek bed.

The two suspected Taliban now lying dead behind us were hiding behind a large boulder. The prisoner also sprang from behind a boulder and now we are approaching another ten-foot rock monster to our front. If there are more Taliban, they will be here. I am not in a risk-taking mood.

"Guidons, I have got a suspected Taliban position to my front. I am going to frag it. So if you hear a 'boom,' don't freak out." Guidons is army talk for "all units."

Gregory replies, "Roger." No one else bothers.

"Siar, cover me," I order as I sling my M4 around onto my back and take out one of my fragmentary grenades. Both the safety pin and safety clip are attached. Both must be removed in order for the spoon to release the striker. This starts the four and a half- to five and a half-second safety fuse, which will culminate in the detonation of the compound that pro-vides the main charge, encased in the deliberately weakened steel casing roughly the size of a pool ball and about the same weight. The clip comes off first, and I firmly grasp the grenade. The boulder is uphill from me, approximately twenty feet away. An easy throw. Throwing grenades up-hill is rarely recommended. But the boulder should keep it from rolling back and will shield me from the blast effects. *Just gotta make sure I clear the boulder.*

I pull the last safety and yell, "Frag out!" as I toss the grenade overhand to the boulder. The grenade clears by only six inches. *That was stupid. But better lucky than good.* Had the grenade hit the boulder, it would have come straight back to me. Since I didn't cook off the grenade by holding it for a few seconds after releasing the last safety, I probably would have had time to scramble to safety, but possibly not.

I wait for what seems like an impossibly long time before the boom is felt and heard and then re-heard through echoes in the valleys. I reclaim my M4 and move quickly around the boulder to discover nothing. *Oh, well. If nothing else, that is a little less weight I have to carry.*

"Dead hole, nothing here," I report over the radio. As I look back, I see four more ANP coming up only a hundred meters behind me. *They made damn good time.* Mahmoud is with them, leading from the front. *Fi-nally, some Afghan leadership.* I am done leading the charge today. I sit with my back against my newly conquered boulder and sip some more water. My anger at the ANP is passing again and I try to be empathetic. Few men of fighting age have failed to suffer from the Taliban at some point in a personal way. They sure didn't become cops because of the good pay and benefits. And a captured Taliban is generally a released Taliban from the unmentored justice ministry jails whose guards are universally recognized as corrupt. I am failing to find outrage now that I think about it. Not that I will allow a prisoner to be harmed while I can control it. *My mission, my rules.* My rules aren't Pashtun rules, though, when it comes to prisoners. Mahmoud comes up to me, showing none of the effects of his near sprint up the hills. *This guy is good,* I say to myself silently.

I look at him and speak directly, allowing Siar to translate at his leisure, "Take your men up the valley and see what you can find. Watch out, there are Taliban all over." He doesn't reply to Siar but firmly barks some orders at the ANP, glaring at the two who were with me before. He then leads the way up the valley confidently. *This isn't his first time to the rodeo.* I fall behind, comfortable with watching the ANP at work. They are moving well and confidently and soon we're approaching a previously hidden orchard with matching ruins. I motion to Siar that I want to take an overwatch position on a small hill to the south that neatly overlooks the ruins. He has recovered from the climb to the point where he makes no argument.

The two of us start traversing the short but steep slope when a sudden explosion jolts me.

"What the fuck was that?" I ask. It wasn't an RPG—not loud enough. It sounded like a grenade, which the ANP don't have. The dust rises 200 meters to the front of the ANP and I realize it was the GP-25, the Soviet version of the M203 rifle-mounted grenade launcher. The ANP are taking no chances and I can't blame them. The ruins are just that and any civilian has already had the opportunity to either flee or surrender.

I reach our spot on the hilltop. We can see clearly all the buildings of the ruins and the surrounding orchards. Hidden from the plains, the spot is absolutely beautiful. A long-neglected but still functioning retaining pool holds a nice but weed-choked pond. The trail continues into the mountains and, I guess, into Naw Bahar. This would be a nice place to hang out for a while. Hidden from view, eating from the mix of almonds and pomegranates. There were once three distinct family compounds here. Although the retaining pond is neglected, the orchards themselves are not. Recently pruned, they show flowers that will bear fruit later. The ANP continue their advance, launching the GP-25 and then checking all the ruins. It is almost fun to watch from up above, and Siar and I chat animatedly about the ANP, the day's events, and the upcoming long drive home.

A burst of fire from several AKs rings out well behind us in the direction of Dhakal and Moore. *What the hell is going on? Are the Taliban counterattacking?*

"Dhakal, what the hell was that?" I ask into the radio, surprisingly calm.

"Sir, the ANP just shot your prisoner." *Well, isn't that just fucking dandy.* Nice to know, especially over the radio. Thank God the Apaches are long gone and unable to hear that little tidbit of joy.

"Roger, ANP test fire." I am long past anger at this point. What the hell am I going to do? I take untrained men into combat. Many of them, if not most, harbor a deep hatred of the Taliban and have joined the police in Zabul Province just for the opportunity to kill them. I am not going to ignore it, however. No, this has to be dealt with formally, with

Sarjang and probably my boss in Kandahar. How far they want to take it is beyond my control. I feel no pity for the man they executed. This guy came to Zabul to kill and maim my comrades. Me as well, if he had the chance. No poor draftee dragged against his will. No uniform. He dressed like a civilian so he could hide behind the innocents in the province and fight when he felt like it. Violating every law of warfare imaginable. *Fuck him.* His death means nothing to me. But I have rules that must be followed. I did my very best to follow them and still failed. What else can I do? I can't stop everything to guard a prisoner that isn't mine in the first place. I had no concept that the ANP would shoot him under the watchful eye of Dhakal and Moore. Even had he lived, he might have been killed later. Either that or released by the justice ministry. Or, if his family had money, maybe by Sarjang.

Stalin once said, "Death solves all problems. No man, no problem." Unfortunately, this has created a whole bunch of problems for me. Problems to be dealt with later, however. At least the guy they killed I know for a fact was Taliban. I have no such certainty about the two dead men lying several hundred meters back in a meandering creek bed. Am I really qualified to judge an Afghan on how he deals with Taliban? Is any American?

The ANP have checked all the ruins and are now circling the orchards looking for Taliban. Their slow pace and repeated searches of the same hut show that there is nothing more to be found and they are going through their paces for my benefit. With the execution of the prisoner, any Taliban left in the valley to the east have dropped their weapons and are probably jogging at a steady pace to Naw Bahar and safety. I am not going to find anybody now. Since the Apaches are gone, no more air support remains that could be useful. An F-16 buzzing around at 10,000 feet above the valley floor at 500 knots sure isn't going to help. Even if the pilot could see a few dismounted Taliban, he couldn't relay that information to me quickly or accurately enough. Nor could he, or would he, drop ordnance on them.

When CAS (close air support) died in 1947, to be briefly resurrected during the Vietnam War before being finally cremated and entombed, so did any chance for extending today's fight. While rotary wing CAS is handy (and the only thing available), it isn't capable of staying overhead for a long period of time like a fixed wing asset. The only real CAS asset left is the AC-130. The air force has fewer than two dozen of these, all of them restricted to flying at night and working only for special operations.

Too bad I fight during the day and there is nothing special about a national guard infantry major running around with a bunch of ANP. All I would really need is a Cessna buzzing around and talking to me on the radio. But those days are long gone. *C'est la guerre nouvelle.*

I take a final look around my hard-earned elevated vantage point. I give a good, long look at the abandoned ruins whose peace will return with our departure. A final glance at the now obviously bored ANP confirms the suspicion that today's Taliban safari has come to a successful, albeit abbreviated, end.

"What do you think, Siar?" I ask.

"That's it, Sir. No more motherfuckers to kill today. Let's go home," he advises.

Never argue with a twenty-two-year-old with an AK, I chuckle to myself as I take a long pull at the nearly empty CamelBak and consider the best way to start our journey home.

The author with his wife and children, before deployment.

The author with an MRAP. The vehicles proved too large and road bound to be useful in actual combat operations.

Afghan police and American mentors in search of Taliban.

The doorways in Zabul were not designed for soldiers in body armor.

The wide, open plains of Zabul gave the Taliban ample warning of our approach.

Afghan National Police (ANP) Chief Sarjang, in his office. Hamid Karzai, then the president of Afghanistan, is featured prominently. Sarjang's Afghan National Army (ANA) counterpart displays the martyred Ahmad Shah Massoud instead.

An Afghan feast. The governor sits at the head of the table while the ANA's commanding general sits to his right and the head of the National Directorate of Security sits to his left.

The author looks out over the Surkhagan Valley from a pile of rocks that was a Taliban machine-gun position.

M.Sgt. Rob Apel shows his exhaustion after two days straight in the Surkhagan. The additional armor he wears shows that he acted as a gunner for the mission.

Soldiers can—and will—sleep anywhere after seventy-two straight hours on mission.

The well-scarred general displays his favorite weapon. How he acquired it remained a mystery.

A completely posed picture showing the ANA and ANP pretending to cooperate. The Tajik-dominated Afghan Army leadership neither trusted nor liked the Pashtun-dominated police.

ANP Deputy Chief Julani, impeccably dressed as always.

The idyllic ruins of Shabazkehl masked by the foothills from the Surkhagan Valley.

Afghan police press the flesh with local farmers.

Motorcycles and Taliban bodies are loaded after the mission.

The charred remains of some of the Apaches' kills.

Gregory, Fahim, and Siar pose with some police while an unidentified Swampfox soldier stands guard in the background.

The IEDs took their toll all too often.

Uniforms and the detritus of battle are burned in place to deny the Taliban any trophies.

The entrancing streams leading to Highway 1 and home.

Afghan police prepare for a long day in the cool of the morning behind a Russian PKM machine gun.

American norms of discretion concerning the enemy dead are absent in Afghan culture.

The "butcher's bill," displayed for the press.

The author studies the map for a later mission while waiting for Afghan army forces to get into position. Cheap cigars were always available in theater.

Sarjang's office in the glow of the filtered afternoon sun.

Sergeant Dhakal enrolls new police officers into the biometric computer, the HIIDE. His knowledge of Urdu proved valuable when Pakistanis were captured.

Sarjang and his staff conduct business in the morning. Chai, chickpeas, and almonds were omnipresent.

The author in a brand-new Ford Ranger.

Homecoming.

7

SURKHAGAN RULES

1427.

"Siar, tell 'em to bring it in," I order.

Siar, his voice nearly gone, wisely uses the ANP radio to send the word out. I still haven't seen or heard from Shah Khan. Not much of the combat leader, it would appear. I'll let Sarjang know when we get home tonight.

"Guidons, Crazy 6. Bring it in and consolidate, we aren't going to catch whatever is still left."

"Roger," Gregory answers.

"Ortiz, did you copy?" More army talk, or actually air force. "Copy" isn't correct radio procedure, but everyone uses it. The air force bowed to the inevitable and uses it as "official speak." The army has yet to follow suit. In a regular unit, I wouldn't use it. But out here and right now, it works and that's enough.

"Ortiz is with me." Gregory again.

"Roger, out."

From my vantage point overlooking the orchards and deserted buildings, I see the ANP start walking back, weapons held by the barrel over the shoulder. I'll have to tone that up when I get down to them. The hill Siar and I climbed with such difficulty is abandoned, and we slide down toward the creek that created the small valley we fought over only a few minutes ago. I hold up at the rock where I thought a hand grenade would be a good idea and, in a few minutes, the five ANP are there with me. Time to collect the two dead guys we left behind and see if they have cell phones or usable intel. The small creek flows swiftly down the fairly steep hill. There are no pools of collected water from natural or man-made dams. The ANP are quiet and I am as well. Everyone thinking his own thoughts.

Going downhill, I carefully watch my step. Bad place to twist an ankle. One of the few advantages of uphill. As my rifle is at the ready, the police have copied me without being told. *Thank heaven for small victories.*

The ANP radio is crackling with Pashto incessantly.

"Siar, what are they talking about?"

"They got the body of a commander they know about and one commander they don't. Plus lots of motorcycles and there are some arguments about who keeps the motorcycles."

"Tell them the Americans get one of the working ones," I remind him. I have plans for it later. Shah Khan had better share them with the guys who actually fought. Another thing to remind Sarjang. The list is growing. If I weren't so emotionally tired, I would be much angrier.

I see the boulder on the side of the hill where those two guys were originally and I know that in another fifty meters or so we should see the bodies, if the ANP haven't moved them. Moment of truth, and the knot in my stomach tightens.

As we turn a bend in the creek, I see them. One of them is moving his arm. *Fuck.*

Dead Taliban I can handle. Prisoners I can handle. Never had a wounded Taliban before. And I sure as hell am not going to let the ANP kill this one. Going to do something right out of this day. But right is hard, and we are going to have to get Ortiz up here with a stretcher and then carry this shit bag down the hill and probably call in a medevac—with Taliban all over the place. What a pain in the ass. *Oh, well.* As we carefully walk closer, the ANP start talking. I scope up and check. The guy just put his hand in his pocket.

Fuck.

No hesitation. The selector rotates again, and I line up the chevron above his ear. The 400-meter stadia line is in the ear and I pull the trigger. No misses this time. The shot hits home and the hand leaves the pocket, empty. I wait ten seconds to see if a grenade goes off. Nothing. I now know I just killed a wounded guy for no good reason. Of course, like everything else in combat, hindsight is perfect, and I had no idea what was in that pocket, if anything. The movement could have been involuntary. The guy has at least one bullet in him and has been lying wounded for at least an hour. He is probably delirious. But it isn't worth the risk. Choose wrong, and I kill five or six of my guys. More frontier arithmetic. Kipling spoke of £2,000 of education dropped to a ten-rupee jezail. The currency and costs might have changed, but the concept remains the same. A

Chinese frag grenade will blow us up as easily as an IED when we are out of the truck and up close. I note silently that usually the ANP would have shot him as soon as he moved. I wonder who they fear more at this point.

As we get closer, I see no indication that these were Taliban. The knot in my stomach tightens more. The ANP won't care and neither will Siar. None of them will tell anyone. But I will know. Forever. There is no time to dwell on it now. If these guys hadn't shot at us, somebody damn close to them did. Military-age males, and neither one wearing the Kandahari hat worn by every male from five to ninety if he doesn't wear a turban. While there's no indication they are Taliban, there's no indication that they're local farmers, either. Circumstantial evidence won't convict on TV, but in the Surkhagan Valley, it's enough for a death penalty. And everybody knows the laws of justice out here on the plains of Zabul. The Surkhagan rules. I followed the rules as best I could by an American sense of right and wrong and still failed. But the combat measure of victory is met. I am alive. And I met the leader's measurement of victory. Every one of my men, American and Afghan, is still alive. One only slightly wounded, and not bad at all. I can, and will, have to deal with the rest.

Across the creek, thirty meters away where Siar and I initially shot the two guys, I can see the folded outlines of the body bags dropped off by the ANP. Time to bag these guys and get back to the HMMWVs.

The rules on this are fairly strict. Non-Muslims (aka Americans) don't touch dead Muslims. So it is on the ANP to put these guys into the body bags. But the guy whose brain I just emptied out of his skull has started to guppy breathe, and the ANP (as well as Siar) are starting to freak the fuck out.

"Guppy breathing"—medically known as agonal respiration—is an involuntary reaction of a dying person. It is recognized by sudden gasping breaths that convulse the upper body and head; the jaw moves with the breaths. In training, I saw it once before in a video. A Lebanese man was executed by an ad hoc firing squad for being an Israeli informant. The guy took twenty shots of AK fire, including one to the head. He then continued to guppy breathe for about ten minutes before it stopped and his body was at last as dead as his brain. While it is going on, it looks like the guy is still alive. Alive with no brain, and that isn't natural. Siar, educated in Kabul, intelligent, has the explanation.

"Sir, he won't die. He is very evil. The *jinns* of Satan are in him. He cannot die." *Jinn* is an Arabic word and used often in the Koran. Jinns are ghosts said to inhabit isolated areas. But they can also possess a body, and clearly now the Afghans think this is the case. I am already pissed off at them and do not have time for this bullshit.

"Siar, tell these guys to shut the fuck up and bag this guy. He is dead; his body is just too fucking stupid to know it," I yell at him.

Siar doesn't bother to translate. "Sir, they won't touch him. If they do, the jinn will enter them."

You gotta to be fucking kidding me! I think. They don't teach this at Fort Riley. I have a several hours' drive out of here, and I still have to get the bodies to Lagman to get them HIIDEd, get the ANP back to Sarjang, and get back to FOB Apache. I am exhausted and angry. The nearest Americans are 400 meters from here but that seems like a universe away. And now I have five Afghans getting louder and more scared and they are losing control. No matter how badly I think the Taliban are beat and running away they could still counterattack, and this hootenanny couldn't fight off a Boy Scout troop.

I am feeling very alone and now I can't even trust Siar to keep his shit together. So, we stand there. *How long?* I don't know. And we look at the man, unarmed and dying. I attempt no first aid. I have no idea how to save a man whose brains are outside of his skull in hundreds of pieces. I have no idea where to start. The ANP wouldn't save him even if it was a simple wound. His eyes are clearly the eyes of a dead man. Vacant, staring, maybe searching for his seventy virgins.

Finally, the great heaving gasps stop to the point where the undead is more dead than alive. I have no more time to waste.

"Siar, tell them to bag this fucking piece of shit now."

"Yes, Sir." And they do. The guppy breathing has stopped. The jaw is still moving a little, but the Afghans now seem to know that whatever evil spirit filled that guy isn't as evil as the American who an hour ago put himself between their guns and a Taliban prisoner. Was it Frederick the Great who said, "They should fear their officers more than they fear the enemy?" *Whatever.*

Disgusted with myself and my inability to again maintain control of my forces, I walk down the creek a bit to be alone and I discover the cache where the dead men hid their radios, cheap but new Chinese ammunition vests, and military style jackets. No matter what I did just a few minutes ago to that dead piece of meat, at least I now know that he and his conventionally killed counterpart were both Taliban and trying to hide that fact from us when we came over the hill. The relief I feel is overwhelming. At no point did I do anything I didn't think was right. But I still had a nagging fear and disgust. Killing a civilian, an innocent man, wasn't something I was prepared to deal with, even if I thought he was a Taliban. I never even considered that it could happen out here.

The Surkhagan rules are too clear. Everybody knows them. Stay in the open. Don't flee. Show your hands. Don't ride your motorcycles in groups of more than two. Simple rules. Fair rules. Fairer than the Taliban's at least. And now, thank God, it turns out these guys died within the Surkhagan rules. I now know this with all certainty and can deal with the rest.

There is still one thing nagging at me and that is the fact that we still haven't found their weapons. The rock where Siar initially indicated they were sits perched above me. Maybe they left them there.

"Siar, let's check out the boulder. I still can't find their fucking AKs."

I try to scramble up, but I lose traction and make no progress. Even traversing, the grade is too steep. I can see the drag marks where the two or three Taliban slid down to the creek to hide from the fire from Siar and me and make good their escape. If they had left the weapons up there, I would have to go around the back side of the hill and then come down the other side. Another 1,200 meters of hard climbing at least. *Fuck that.* The radios, vests, and ammunition are enough.

Siar can't make it either, and he isn't nearly as loaded down as I am. I am out of water as well. The first guy is bagged. I grab a handle with Siar and two ANP and we start making our way downhill toward the HMMWV, water, Americans, and sanity. I hope that what happened in this narrow valley, in the foothills of the Sur Ghar Mountains, above the Surkhagan Valley, and just outside a rubble pile known as Surkay Tangay stays in this valley forever. It is time to leave, carrying a body I shot two separate times. The dead weight digging into my hands through the straps serves as my hair shirt and I hope it will be penance enough.

Previously I could avoid where the trail crossed the stream by jumping across. Now, with the additional weight and tethered by the body bag to three other men, this proves impossible and my feet are quickly soaked. The boots I wear have drain holes built into them. So, while my socks are soaked, I don't have to worry about the water pooling in the boots. The body bag itself is not zippered all the way. The Taliban's blood is pouring out one side and onto me. I drop my corner and zip up the bag all the way. I quickly walk over to the stream and wash the blood off as best I can. Walking back, I pick my corner of the body bag back up. No one has said a word. The coupled magazines in my pocket are still banging against my leg. *Never again. Too much of a pain in the ass.* A lot of lessons learned today.

My arms are aching. The rigid poles of a stretcher provide some structural relief to the load, and a live body will naturally use the core muscles of the abdomen and back to stay straight even when wounded. But dead weight is just that. The load is pulling unnaturally at my arms and shoulders, and between that and my body armor, the lactic acid is building up. The bag is half dragging in the mud and the rocks, which tear a hole. More blood leaks out onto the ground.

Finally, I can see the HMMWV. Dhakal is still dutifully in the turret, the barrel of the .50-cal pointed toward the hills we just came from. Moore is out of the driver's seat. His helmet is off but his attention, and rifle, are trained forty-five degrees off from Dhakal. *Good enough.*

"Moore! Get over here! Help the ANP with the other body," I yell out. Moore seems relieved to be moving. I pick up my step to get to the ANP Ranger and drop the body. My arm aches.

"Dhakal, you OK?"

"Yeah, fine, bored. How about you, Sir?"

"Thirsty, tired. What happened with the prisoner?"

"I don't know, Sir. I was facing the mountains when it happened."

"Fair enough. Where is the wounded guy?"

Dhakal points to the ANP Ranger loaded with motorcycles and body bags. The policeman has a bandage across his cheek with very little blood showing. Obviously, a scratch. He is smiling broadly. Pashtun bravery has been proven. He will probably get a motorcycle for his troubles and a little extra cash for getting wounded. A day well spent. I smile back at him and pat him on the back. *"Manana,"* I say. Good. He gets the idea.

Moore stumbles up with his own dead-weight burden. Security is good enough, and the Ranger is being loaded with the last two bodies. I take my helmet and body armor off to take a break. It takes three and a half bottles of water to refill my CamelBak, so I take the remaining half bottle to drink now. Getting back to the HMMWV is calming. Compared to the Surkhagan hills, it is practically home. I see several BFT messages from Zabul, Hoplite (my headquarters in Kandahar), and Rob. All asking for the same thing. SITREP. Situational report, aka what the hell is happening.

Sitting down, I thankfully remove the damn coupled magazines from my pocket and I think about what to type. The BFT format is not the best for relaying all the details and nuances of combat. The less said, the better. The details can come later when I get my story straight. It takes three minutes to think of the reply and thirty seconds to type it: "Pursuit over. Consolidating. 1 ANP WIA. UNK enemy KIA." That's how I summarize the past few hours.

While I'm typing, Gregory and Ortiz come up with Fahim. Sweaty but smiling. I get out, and handshakes are exchanged. These two were all over the hills to my north, chasing ghosts. They found many of the Taliban killed by the Apaches, but they couldn't chase down any others. The three guys we got were probably pushed by Gregory's and Ortiz's ANP.

"You guys OK?" I ask.

"Yeah, good. We out of here?" Ortiz asks.

"Yeah, just got to get everybody together."

Still sitting on the hood of the HMMWV, I grab the hand mic on my vest. "Swampfox 7, Crazy 6. Where are you?"

"At the orchard with the burned-out motorcycle."

I peek into my HMMWV and zoom in the map on the BFT. The map data still isn't good enough so I reload the satellite photo imagery. It takes the computer a while to transition from topographic to photo image. Meanwhile Ortiz and Gregory are pilfering my water bottles from the back of the HMMWV. They are both smiling broadly.

Gregory suddenly says, "I so want to head-butt you right now."

I have no idea what he means by that. *Is he angry?* I don't think so. Maybe a legacy from his football days. When you're wearing a helmet, head-butting is motivational, but neither of us is wearing one at the moment. Considering that Gregory is about eight inches taller and fifty pounds heavier than I am, I am glad he doesn't go with his instincts. Still. *Head-butting? New generation.* I suddenly feel old.

I grab a case of water and start handing out bottles to the ANP. Half of them drink it while the other half remove their boots and wash their feet with it. I have seen them countless times wash their feet with bottled water and then drink from a random stream, so I rarely give out water to the Afghans, but today was different, even if their actions weren't. There are some aspects of Afghan culture I doubt I will ever decipher. While we avoid dropping trash on missions, the Afghans have no qualms about throwing the water bottles onto the ground. Maybe they need a crying faux Indian commercial to let them in on the sins of littering. Or maybe pollution guilt is a luxury for the spoiled westerner. They never save water I give them. It is used instantly. Less to carry. They quickly get back to task.

Under the shade of an unidentified tree, the last of the bodies and motorcycles are loaded into the back of the Ranger. I check the BFT and the satellite photo has uploaded. The blue icon identifying Gregory's and Genovese's HMMWVs are seen along the same wadi we took into Surkay Tangay. Time to bring everyone back together. I still haven't seen Shah Khan, despite the fact that we drove in from Abdul Qadir Kalay together. Ortiz jumps into the spare seat in my vehicle while Gregory and Fahim find room amid three motorcycles, four dead bodies, and two additional ANP in the back of the Ranger.

The joke is old but so very true:

"How many ANP can you fit into a Ranger?"

"One more."

As we crawl along the road I don't bother to put my helmet or my headset on. Our speed is in deference to the load carried by the ANP Ranger following me. The terrain slowly becomes flatter and more inhospitable. The occasional trees give way to lone trees until no vegetation exists except for scrub and wheat. The chassis of the HMMWV creaks as I check the BFT's screen and clear out a few more messages. One message tells me that the two Taliban engaged by the returning Apaches have been found, but the message isn't clear whether it was ANP or Romanians who picked them up. Nomad never got there. I am not sure what they did today, but their BFT icons show them off-road near Highway 1. Gray is doing his thing; might as well leave him be. The two Taliban must have been only wounded by the Apaches as they were apparently found in a Kuchi camp. Either the Kuchis helped them or they made it there on their own. The official story on the BFT message is that they were dead when the ANP showed up. *Yeah. Sure they were.* But that is how it's going today. I hazard to guess they bled out. That will be the official story, at least.

Ahead I see the rest of the Rangers and the two HMMWVs. The positioning is haphazard and not very good defensively. I'm going to let it ride for now and discuss it later. Taliban got their ass beat today; they aren't coming back for a while.

There is a lone body bag next to a burnt-out motorcycle. I climb out to take a look. The motorcycle has strewn burnt cartridges and the ammunition belt distinctive to a PKM. *Yeah, definitely Taliban.* I take some closeup pictures of the burnt-out hulk and the 7.62X54R casings in case anyone has any doubts. The motorcycle is right next to a low wall that borders a wheat field. The wall is topped with the branches of a thorny brush that serves as ample substitute for barbed wire. I can see where the wall is partially toppled by either 30mm fire or the Taliban attempting to get over it. Maybe both.

Since the camera is out, I take some trophy pictures. Now, a foot on a body bag could be construed as distasteful, so it's a foot on the burned-out motorcycle with the body bag not so discreetly in the background. I hand the camera to Gregory and Fahim. Siar and a few ANP surround me for the shot. My anger is well disguised and quickly disappearing as I realize that everyone is safe and we'll be going home soon. A few more cameras are passed around and the shot repeated.

Pretty much everyone is relaxed and most have lost their body armor. Ordinarily in the Surkhagan, I would be chewing ass, but not now. Right now we own this whole fucking valley. The Taliban know it, the Afghans who live here know it, my ANP know it, and other Americans and I sure as hell know it. Owned, as the younger soldiers would say on the internet. And it is a damned good feeling.

The feeling is going to linger because the ANP are fixing a broken wheel on a Ranger. They've stacked up some rocks to give the pitiful jack a little more lift and they're using bailing wire to secure the front axle to the frame. It's either that or we leave it behind, and that isn't going to happen.

"Siar, tell Shah Khan to let me know when he is ready."

"No problem, Sir."

I walk around and shake hands with all the US and police. While all seem happy, the fatigue is showing through. I am certainly feeling it as well. The hunger is gnawing, too. Gregory is checking out a blood-soaked turban taken from one of the Taliban. His finger waggles through a bullet hole. He smiles. It's a good day. We finally caught the ghosts and punished them. Payback for a lot of ANP and Romanians. I look forward to seeing the Romanian commander tonight. I take a final, satisfied look around and head back to the HMMWV.

Reaching the HMMWV, I pop open the trunk to grab an MRE. I haven't eaten a whole one since I got in country eight months earlier. I'm not going to start now, but maybe I'll luck out and grab a few edible things to munch on. The HMMWV hatch is a pain to open but easier than previous incarnations. Technically it's a push down and a pull to open, but the hinges need constant oiling to work properly. Luckily, this one has been oiled and it promptly opens. The five empty body bags stored in the back are all taken. The ammo remains untouched; we haven't shot that many crew-served weapons. I find the dusty box of MREs and grab a couple to hand out. I offer one to Dhakal and Moore, who both decline. Apparently, they have been munching while I was scurrying across the hills. I tear one open and quickly discard the main entrée. I find some Reese's Pieces—good enough for now. Pound cake, too. That's edible. That should hold me over till we get back to FOB Apache.

I cruise back to the BFT, and still more messages are flashing. I have time to take better stock. So while still eating, I get back out and start counting bodies and motorcycles. Of the five trucks, each has its share of motorcycles and body bags. I count ten motorcycles and eight body bags. *Not a bad haul.* Maybe a few more from the Apaches. I start checking with Geno. Three of the bodies were there when they showed up. Two of them were from Geno's and Gregory's trucks from the M240s. Three are from my crew in the stream bed. The Apaches fired for a long time; there must be more bodies in the hills I don't see. Something else to fix when we get back. Gotta figure out a way to mark the locations of who they shoot. Maybe collect some more cell phones and luck out with Pakistan ID cards. The important thing is that at the end of the fight, I own the battlefield and the bodies, not the Taliban.

I check with Shah Khan through Fahim, who is also wandering about. I get the rundown of weapons. The broken-stock PKM has been exchanged with a Taliban one that is in better shape. The ANP are claiming that the Taliban had a lot of AMD-65s, the standard ANP issue. This is bullshit, but worth it. The fact is the Chinese and Russian AKs that the Taliban use are much better than the Hungarian ones issued to the ANP. Frankly, I don't care as long as we can wing it when it comes to accountability. I'll have to work with the civilian mentors to fix the books. Shouldn't be a problem. The Afghans haven't really earned these as trophies, but they will claim them as such.

In an earlier time in an earlier war, I would be bringing back an AK for myself. From World War I to Vietnam, a combat veteran could expect to bring back a weapon from a fallen enemy. Often those who weren't in combat would trade for one or purchase one to take back, to make the war stories better. Now we can't even send an old license plate home. Souvenirs taken from the battlefield are seen as too aggressive—like we are fighting an enemy or something. But I can buy all the souvenirs I want at the bazaars in KAF. It is one of the unwritten laws that the farther away you are from the fighting, the more souvenirs you obtain. Maybe it is boredom. *Gotta do something sitting around the giant FOB. Let's shop!* Back at home, I would see guys' offices that were covered floor to ceiling with rugs, trinkets, plaques, framed flags, etc. Now I know that those guys spent sixty days in Kuwait and never left the air conditioning. On the other hand, I know guys with three tours that have nothing on their walls at all.

Because the truck still isn't repaired, I have the time to tap a longer message on the BFT:

> 8 bodies recovered at Surkay Tangay.
>
> 10 motorcycles. Multiple RPGs, PKMs, and AKs.
>
> 3 ICOMs, cell phones, ammunition, and hand grenades.
>
> 1 ANP lightly wounded, no evacuation required. SP from current location in approx 30 minutes.

The feast of killing complete, I start doing the after-dinner math. Timelines aren't as critical, but it's good to keep track. It's 1430 now. Three-hour drive to the highway, thirty minutes from the highway to Lagman. *Home by dinner and before dark. Score!*

Dhakal is walking about and Moore is taking a leak against the front wheel well—the urinal of choice for most soldiers. I suddenly realize I haven't gone to the bathroom, nor needed to, since I woke up this morning. Time to drink more water. Again sparing the now-replenished CamelBak, I grab a water bottle from the back seat. The middle of the HMMWV is a raised deck on which sits an ammo rack, the seat belt, and radios. It is littered with .50-caliber cases and empty water bottles. Having the time, I sweep the refuse of combat to the floorboards to be cleaned later but at least provide a safe spot for Dhakal to stand for the four remaining hours to get home.

I'm always amazed at the discipline of the gunners, who stand all day in fifty to sixty pounds of armor (gunners wear extra) without complaint. While walking creates its own stresses, gunning is tough business. You're never able to stretch or sit. There are benches that can be hooked up for gunners, but I haven't seen them in my trucks. So stand they must until the mission is complete.

Dhakal returns, chewing on something and smiling. He got a few hero shots in as well. This is a good day for pictures. Moore wanders about with intent to do the same. Siar enters the HMMWV and plops down, exhausted. He, too, grabs a bottle of water.

"Sir, I am fucking tired," Siar exclaims. "Fuck" is universally known as the first word learned by Afghans, its flexibility being useful among soldiers from any nation.

"Me, too. Any idea how much longer with the Ranger?" I inquire.

"I think they are almost finished. Give me a minute and I'll check."

Rehydrated and rested, emails answered, and stomach satiated, if not completely full, I figure now would be a good time to get everybody refocused. I crawl out of the HMMWV and bring everyone together.

"Good job today, guys. Remember, we still have to get home. I don't think they want any piece of us right now, but we don't know for sure. Rotate drivers and gunners if you have to; we need people awake and alert. I figure four more hours and we are home. Let's not fuck this up now. Questions?"

Fahim is nearby so I grab him instead of Siar and watch as the Afghans lower the Ranger they have repaired. I crawl down and inspect the handiwork. It will work, if we drive slow enough. I smile at Shah Khan and tell him "good job" through Fahim. My earlier anger and frustration have largely dissipated, though not entirely. But now isn't the time to deal with that. Shah Khan isn't a strong leader, but I still need him to get home safely. Chewing him out now wouldn't be beneficial and could be negative. *Later.* Besides, I will tell Sarjang, who will most certainly know better how to deal with him than I will. Maybe he will do nothing. And maybe that's OK. Zabul can be confusing.

I tell Shah Khan I don't care how we get out of here, as long as we take a different, shorter route home. He nods his understanding as Fahim interprets the request. How I would execute this fight without the Afghan knowledge is a mystery. The maps can't tell me what the locals already know. Today wouldn't have happened without them, that is for sure.

Once again, the anachronistic order of "Mount up!" is given in English and Pashto. Body armor is thrown on, with a slightly slower cadence than seven hours earlier. The gunners are slower to ease their way down into their cupolas. I sit down in the HMMWV and put my headphones back on. Before donning my own armor, I turn off the radio on my back. Shouldn't need it again today.

"VIC 1, REDCON 1."

"VIC 2, REDCON 1."

"VIC 3, REDCON 1."

Small miracles, we all got it right.

Shah Khan, for all his lack of appearances in the fight today, still takes lead on the way out. I can't call him a coward. He moves down the trail back toward the village of Surkhagan and eventually to Highway 1. We all follow in line, the heavily laden Rangers' rear suspensions sagging with bodies and trophies from today's battle.

8

9-LINE

1545.
Although driving to Surkay Tangay through Surkhagan was laden with risk, one advantage of having taken that risk is that the route back through Abdul Qadir Kalay is now clear, so we make good time. The convoy is traveling at about twenty kilometers per hour; the vehicle spacing increases because of the dust. Within a few minutes we're back in Surkhagan and the town is alive. I guess they, too, know the fight is over. It is good to be a winner, judging from the waves and smiles, which before were usually absent from what villagers I could see.

Dhakal waves back from behind the .50-cal. "Sir, looks like they like us now," he needlessly informs me.

"Either that or we scared the shit out of them."

"Hadn't thought of it that way," he admits.

"Me neither, until now." We pass through the same wadi running through the center of town that serves as the main street and, during the rainy season, becomes a river. The rock-strewn bed cuts the dust down to a manageable level. Geno notes the villagers' newfound friendliness as well.

"Sure, now they fucking love us."

"No shit," agrees Gregory. I have been in three TICs in this village and two other missions as well, probably half as many as the guys from Swampfox. We have never seen this reaction. If we saw anybody at all, it was a brief glance from behind a quickly closed compound gate. These people live by the Surkhagan rules. It is hard to blame them. While the International Security Assistance Force/Afghan National Security Forces (ISAF/ANSF) and the Taliban have all agreed that this is the battlefield of choice in eastern Zabul, I doubt the villagers even had a vote. And why would they? They don't need any of us. The constant stream combined with well water ensures a good mixture of wheat and orchards. There is no poppy growing that I know of. Even if there were, the scale would be such that it would only augment their income rather than being a cash crop. It is a beautiful town, similar to Shabazkehl, but larger. The surrounding hills have a few orchards and some ruins, whereas Shabazkehl had ruins in the flats and the occupied huts in the hills. I had assumed that today the fight would be in Surkhagan because previously that was where the Taliban would always flee. Maybe they thought they would try something different but didn't realize the Apaches and ISR would catch them trying a new route. *Flexibility.* I think that is the word for it. Not a bad idea on their part, but this time we had the surprises.

I see the kids out and the women in the burkas flaunting their T&A. Toes and ankles. I am glad—relieved, even—that the fight pushed north. Had the Taliban fled into Surkhagan and held up in the village, the fight wouldn't have been canceled. It would have gone on. The Apaches would have tracked them into huts and probably dropped a Hellfire there. All within the laws of warfare. And we still would have driven up, with our .50-cals and automatic grenade launchers. It would have been messier with a lot more risk both to the villagers and the ANP— not to mention me! Give the Taliban credit for that. It could have ended with destroyed buildings and civilian deaths with much crying and agony. All because the civilians were born in a village that gives name to the most contested piece of real estate in Zabul. But all of that was avoided because the Taliban commander, quite possibly dead now, decided to avoid Surkhagan and go, for the first time I am aware of, to Surkay Tangay. Did he know about the helicopters from his spies in Qalat and make that change to protect the people? Was it dumb luck? Was it trying to trick us by retreating a new way? Yet again, a definitive answer escapes me. And, yet again, I am just fine with that. No civilians on the battlefield? I will take that fight every time. It should always be so simple; a straight-up fight with minimal civilian casualty potential isn't easy to find any more. So the people of Surkhagan are smiling and waving and going back to their fields. We quickly leave a peaceful, friendly, and crowded Surkhagan behind us as we pick up speed and kick up more dust again. I wonder what it will be like next time I come back. The Taliban are certain to return, and so are we.

It has only been ten minutes since we left Surkay Tangay, and we are through Surkhagan and moving back to Abdul Qadir Kalay. Between Surkhagan and Abdul Qadir Kalay there is a distinctive dome to the north of the road. It dominates the entire valley and is deserted. *A good place for a*

COP if I had ten times more police and mentors, I think to myself. Swampfox has used it for target practice before while driving back from fruitless, but dangerous, missions. Good place to watch the effects of MK-19 40mm grenades as well as to relieve some of the frustration of driving all day for nothing. There have been Kuchis along its bottom edge at times, but not today. At the maneuver training centers in Fort Irwin, California, and Hohenfels, Germany, there is always a distinctive, isolated terrain feature. If the Surkhagan were a training center, this would have a nifty nickname. "Old Baldy." "The Dome." "Belly Hill." Something like that. Every time we drive through here, I see it as decisive terrain from my previous incarnation as a late-to-the-party cold warrior preparing to defend the Fulda Gap. But now it is just an intellectual exercise; a problem for the student to solve.

In Afghanistan, traditional well-defendable terrain is of questionable value for either side. For the good guys, it just means we are static and can be screwed with and attacked if we show weakness, mortared for good measure even if we're not weak. For the bad guys, it means they are static and will get found and JDAMed (joint direct attack munition, a 2,000-pound guided bomb). The decisive terrain in this fight is the ratline. Mobility. Maintaining our movement while denying his. I use Apache helicopters, he uses IEDs; the objective is the same. Fix him in place. Smart Taliban never fix themselves by staying static. I have to make them stay still by flying over their heads and scaring the shit out of them. They try to scare the shit out of me with IEDs. I realize both sides are successful. IEDs are effective because even when we are mobile, we're often nearly worthless. The MRAP (mine-resistant ambush-protected vehicle) is roadbound, for all intents and purposes. In Iraq—and Afghanistan is just the bastard stepson to Iraq as far as the United States is concerned—roadbound might be OK: Don't die while driving and get out and kill bad guys, who are usually located less than one kilometer from a paved road. But in Afghanistan, paved roads are hard to come by. If the enemy can keep you in your MRAPs, he has taken away your mobility in his terrain. I know the Taliban doesn't use Highway 1 most of the time. They run the unpaved, unmapped ratlines, just like the ones that go through this valley. Sure, a hilltop is key once the fight starts, but holding it before or after a fight doesn't help. We have to stay there. But even if we do stay, the Taliban just go around us. Like water around a big rock in a stream. So really the COP idea would be nice simply because we are ten minutes from Surkhagan and not four hours. That alone would be worth it.

Because the fight is over and we have driven this stretch of road before, the entire vibe is different. We are still on edge and looking everywhere. The Taliban are all over the place right now, that is for sure. I have no doubt the call has gone out for help and the part-timers have grabbed their AKs, prepared for action. We have the ass and the attitude, so I highly doubt they will start anything. But that doesn't change the fact that forty guys with rifles are probably looking at our patrol and watching for weakness. I am determined not to show any.

Moving west in the afternoon sun and dust is proving to be a pain. Visibility drops even further, and the convoy spreads out more. Dhakal is caked in dust, but fortunately he's turned to the side covering his sector of fire and isn't facing directly into the sun. Moore is doing well and has been surprisingly stoic the whole day. Tired, more mature, angry, or scared could be the explanation; a combination thereof is most likely.

In another fifteen minutes we make it back to Abdul Qadir Kalay. The sun gives the whole village a glow that was absent in the harsher light of the late morning. The other difference is that Abdul Qadir Kalay is as deserted as Surkhagan was crowded. Is this because the villagers are scared because the Taliban were meeting here? Obviously, the village supports the Taliban, otherwise they wouldn't have met there. I wonder if the villagers think we are going to do something to them in retribution. Of course, I wouldn't, but if the ANP weren't with us, would they do something? Maybe. But then again, if we weren't with the ANP, they almost assuredly wouldn't have come out to Surkhagan in the first place. *It's complicated.* We plow quickly through Abdul Qadir Kalay, and I involuntarily relax a little as we're now out in the open. While confined to the village, RPGs and AKs really can't miss. But out of the village our visibility is great, and we can see far enough that I know they couldn't hit us if they tried.

The ANP are leading, as they should be, and I'm curious to see which way they're going. Out of Abdul Qadir Kalay the road divides and the ANP have two ways to get back to Highway 1. The northern cut takes us to the town of Duri, where Rob was in his mess of a fight recently. The southern cut takes us to the town of Ebrahimkhel.

The ANP convoy swings south. Two earlier fights had made the Taliban leery of gathering too close to Highway 1 to prep for their missions. So, Ebrahimkhel stopped being a main gathering point for Taliban, making their final journey to Highway 1 that much longer. The town is identical to most of the others along the well-traveled trail. A nearby spring gives it a large combination of orchards and wheat fields, and the adjacent hamlets and villages are all fairly clean. In the five kilometers between Abdul Qadir Kalay and Ebrahimkhel there are seven populated villages and two deserted ones. But the local stream dries up and a dried wadi is all we have for company for another ten kilometers until we reach Highway 1. *Almost home.*

The trail we have been taking now dives into a wadi—a superhighway of dirt road over a hundred meters in width. The annual floods regularly sweep the loose dirt away, and a pebble- and rock-strewn quasi-road meanders to our front. The ANP have to slow down a bit as they maneuver to avoid large rocks and irregularities in the wadi. This wadi is so large it has even been bestowed with a name: Duri Mandeh. After the first kilometer in the isolated desert, off the constricted and easily mined road, I relax even more and, for the first time, the lack of sleep really hits me. I am physically and mentally exhausted. Weighing heavily on me is how to handle the executed prisoner in the inevitable upcoming paperwork, my own frustration at the lack of control I exhibited, and the shooting of the wounded Taliban. I am not sure how much I would have changed, aside from firing into the dirt on the dash to Surkhagan.

With those thoughts, combined with the physical exertion from humping the hills while being shot at (albeit ineffectively), I simply cannot keep my eyes open. The radios are silent. Moore and Dhakal are focused on their tasks. The BFT is fairly quiet. I can't hear the SATCOM over the headset and the sound of the HMMWV. The creaking and rocking and heat are all combining. A sip of warm water does nothing to awaken me. My right arm presses against the three-inch-thick glass, and I prop my face on my hand. My eyelids get heavier. It has been a long day. I need to get some chewing tobacco before I pass out.

I see it, hear it, and feel it at the same time. An impossibly loud thunderclap in the nearly cloudless sky and the plume of dirt funneling straight up. A clearly identifiable wheel and a nearly unidentifiable body arc to the left. The rumble across the parched wadi and through the wheels of my UAH bounce the several-ton vehicle a few inches. The ANP Ranger immediately to my front rears back like a frightened horse, impossibly contorted. The men in the back are slowly thrown off. The truck falls back down with the front of the vehicle stretched to the sky, the driver's door at the apex over the roll bar between the back seat and the bed of the truck.

"IED! IED!" comes across the net from several voices, simultaneously and needlessly.

I am awake now. The Taliban have regained my complete and undivided attention.

"Dhakal, cover the nine o'clock. Moore, move to the left of the wreckage, cover that side," I quickly order over the internal intercom.

I can't do anything about the people in the truck this second. The first rule in responding to IEDs is to ensure nobody else gets killed. While the terrain isn't optimum for a complex ambush (IED followed up with small arms), I am not taking chances. As the medics are going to be working (I hope!) on wounded, I want to surround the site with armored vehicles. With only three armored vehicles, I can only cover so much. The twelve o'clock position is wide open and clear, and the three trucks in front of the stricken vehicle are already there.

"Geno, take the three o'clock. Gregory take the six. Dismounts out, Ortiz up," I push across the net. No complexities here; this is a battle drill, unfortunately. A reflexive action. I grab the handset for the satellite phone. Someone is already on there. I listen for a few seconds to see how critical it is. All of eastern Afghanistan shares the net. Despite the fact that I probably have a mix of dead and wounded, I still may not be in the direst circumstances right now. The conversation turns out to be mundane, however. They can wait. Right now the war is going to revolve around my men. My vehicle still hasn't even stopped moving.

"Break, break, Zabul Base, Crazybear 6, requesting immediate medevac, over." The break tells everyone on the net to shut up. The medical evacuation is a standardized report consisting of nine lines. The nine-line medevac. It will take at least fifteen minutes before the medevac crew will be ready. So even without all the details, I need to get the helicopters ready as soon as possible.

I can imagine the hearts dropping in TOCs all across Afghanistan. I have been there. An American patrol is requesting immediate help. Someone has been at least hurt, possibly killed. I have heard the panicked cries or the calm request. Sometimes we still hear the rattle and boom of RPGs being fired as the guy on the ground tries to unfuck the impossible situation. This isn't the first time I have had to do it. I try my damndest to sound as calm as possible.

"Crazybear 6, Zabul Base, Send it."

I look on the BFT screen and tap the upper right corner with the attached stylus. The date and time change to my immediate location. There are fifteen digits pinpointing my location in the world. I only need eight right now, so I edit it to the essentials. Taped to the window is a copy of the report format. This is not something I want to be scrambling for when I need it.

"Line 1. Uniform Alpha 300672." This is where I am. They need this.

"Line 2. 56.125." This is my radio frequency. The helicopters have the same type of radios we do. When they get close enough, we will talk using this frequency. The Apaches used the same frequency earlier today.

"Lines 3–9 to follow, over." The rules are they need the first five lines to launch the mission. But I don't know the rest yet. The most important thing right now is to get them moving and get the helicopters started.

"Crazybear 6, Zabul Base, copy all. What happened?" The question is extraneous but fair; they need info. If we are in an ambush, they may be gearing up a QRF (quick reaction force). Ordinarily, the unit would request one, but men under fire can lose their heads, so Zabul is making sure and getting as much info to the medevac pilots as possible in the process. Medevacs don't like to fly into the middle of an active firefight, but I have no doubt they will if we ask. Balls of steel. Not bad for pilots, I guess. Flying around in an armored tank like the Apache is one thing. Landing in the middle of the desert and being a big unarmored target is something else entirely. I don't want the job, that's for sure.

"IED, no small arms right now, securing LZ," I answer. It's all I know right now.

"Roger, medevac crews notified, Zabul Base out." It's a slight breach of radio etiquette for the noninitiating station to end the conversation with "out." But it's the right thing here. They know I'm busy and they aren't going to bother me anymore. Nothing more I can do in the truck. Time to assess the damage.

I take off my headset and grab my rifle. Pushing the steel door open again, I check my footing. Although it's not a common practice in Afghanistan, a favorite trick is to sprinkle smaller, man-targeting IEDs around larger ones. Not that I necessarily would see them, but that's the training and it can't hurt. It looks OK, so I plant my foot and look around. Ortiz has taken off his body armor and is working on a casualty. Gregory is out checking ANP, pulling security and waving them forward. Fahim is with Ortiz and talking to the patient. I can't see much around the huddle, but assume it is bad. Two ANP lie unmoving but apparently uninjured next to the truck—probably the guys who got thrown out of the back of the vehicle. The ANP from the other trucks have spread out in all directions except the nine o'clock, which Dhakal is supposed to be covering. But

I notice Moore hasn't moved the truck in the right location and is still behind the destroyed truck and not beside it.

I grab Gregory, who turns on the radio on my back.

"Moore, nine o'clock, cover the truck," I order over the net.

Because of the IED, I suspect he is a bit gun-shy about moving farther. Regardless, he creeps the truck forward. Dhakal is covering the right sector with the .50-cal. *I wish the Taliban would try something now.* I am back in my angry phase.

Security is OK, medics are working. Time to get the rest of the situation and update Zabul Base. I need the casualty count.

As Moore pulls forward I see an indeterminate, though unnatural, blob about seventy-five meters away from the destroyed truck. I half jog over to check it out. Checking stuff out shouldn't be a priority, but no one is covering this side and I need to do it if no one else is. As I get closer, I see the now-filthy gray of an ANP tunic. Filling it is half of an ANP.

I recognize him. He was the guy I ordered to take the prisoner back. I had walked with him all day, but never got his name. *Karma is a bitch.* He is neatly severed at navel level. His arms and head are still attached but his pelvis and legs are nowhere to be seen. He certainly didn't suffer. There is no blood that I can see. The heart shut down immediately. So did the brain. His eyes have the same open, vacant stare I saw a few hours ago in the enemy's face. It's a metaphysical change. While it's a body, it is no longer a man. Just meat. I feel nothing but the still building anger at the unseen Taliban responsible.

So that's what I saw when the IED went off. The truck that got hit carried the ANP who were with me at Surkay Tangay. Simplifies what I am going tell Sarjang about the prisoner. Allah took care of the problem for me. *C'est la guerre.* There is nothing to check, no first aid to render and, without taking a knee or a second thought, I turn and walk quickly back to the truck to get the rest of the casualty count. On the way, I see half a foot. I hope it belonged to the same guy I just left. He won't be needing it.

I come to the truck first—mangled, the driver's side higher than the passenger side. Both front seats are still attached, somehow. The left front wheel is completely missing; no evidence at all it ever existed save a severed axle. Left front wheel hit a pressure plate. No command wires, most likely. God only knows how long this IED has been patiently waiting for someone to drive across it. Weeks? Days? Hours? The severed body I abandoned was probably driving. I hope he was. If that wasn't the driver then I doubt we will ever find that body.

The bed of the truck is almost unblemished. Still loaded with motorcycles and body bags. The two stunned ANP I saw earlier are lying quiet but smiling. In shock and temporarily deafened, but they should be OK. Coming around the right side of the truck, I see and smell the growing puddle of diesel under where the passenger seat should be, but isn't. The engine is gone, but the transmission is still visible. The passenger seat is practically in the empty lap of the back seat. The crew compartment is so mangled I think there must be three or four dead. The only guys who could possibly have lived would be the two in the bed of the truck.

Ortiz is now by himself with the casualty, and I have to figure out his status. I almost have all the information needed to finish the medevac request. I don't know where Fahim and Geno are. I also don't know where Siar is. That can wait.

"Ortiz, what's up?"

"Sir, I need another tourniquet," he says quickly, loudly but calmly. As opposed to the dead driver, this guy is very much alive and very much covered in blood, as is Ortiz. I reach down to my right ankle pocket and grab my tourniquet, dropping it next to Ortiz. I mentally note to grab another from my HMMWV when I finish the medevac request. I notice that Ortiz, in his haste, isn't wearing protective nitrile gloves.

"Ortiz, glove up," I tell him.

"Sir!?" This time he yells, annoyed. But the tone is clear: *I am trying to save a life here and you are fucking with me about gloves?*

I don't say anything else and he quickly calms down. He pours sterile water over his hands and quickly puts his gloves on and keeps working.

"You need anything else?"

"No, Sir. Thanks." The "thanks" sounds legit. Whether from the request for help or the reminder to worry about his own safety as well as his patient's, I don't know.

OK. One KIA, one lightly wounded, one seriously fucked up. Time to get the follow-up report to Zabul Base.

It has been three minutes.

I pass by the mangled truck en route to my own and see Geno working on another ANP I hadn't seen, somehow.

"Geno, what's up?"

"Nothing. This guy is going to be OK." One look confirms the assessment. Geno takes more than a normal passing interest in first aid and is pretty capable. Ortiz has his hands full now and, despite his denial, he could probably use the help.

"When you are done, go help Ortiz. I think he needs it."

"No problem," he replies without looking up. I note that while not awash in bodily fluids, Geno, too, is without his gloves.

"Glove up," I tell him.

"Don't have any," he replies. I break open my own pouch, where I keep a couple of pairs of gloves. I hand two to him and he puts them on without a word. *At least he didn't tell me to shut up. Making progress.* So the count is now four WIA and one KIA. It is quiet; chances are the Taliban weren't even watching this spot.

I walk back to the UAH and open the door. Leaning over without sitting down I grab the hand mic again to the SATCOM. I wait a few seconds to see if anyone is talking. Quiet.

"Zabul Base, Crazybear 6. Stand by for remainder of medevac request, over."

"Roger, send it."

"Line 3. 1 Bravo, 3 Charlie." Line 3 tells the birds what to expect as far as seriousness when they get there. Do they need a doctor on board? What is the timeline? Are we the priority? Alpha indicates urgent. Bravo indicates both urgent and requiring surgery. Ortiz's patient clearly is a Bravo, the most serious. Charlie is a priority patient. Needs help, but will live for a while without it. Delta and Echo are routine and convenience, respectively. Please come if you can find the time. But my report means serious shit. A Bravo patient on line 3 means if you don't hurry, this guy is going to die.

"Line 4. Delta." This is a request for special equipment. Depending upon terrain or wounds, we might need a special litter, a hoist or, in this case, a ventilator. While the guy I saw seemed to be breathing OK, the severity of the wounds indicates that any little bit will help. The medevac birds carry a ventilator, regardless.

"Line 5. Four Litter." While maybe they can walk, I am not sure. So everybody is on a stretcher or litter, in military speak. This line tells whether they are the walking wounded or not. A standard medevac bird can carry four wounded on litters, so not an issue.

"Line 6. Echo." This is the code for the enemy situation. While the Taliban aren't doing anything, they are probably watching. They will definitely be watching by the time the medevac helicopter gets there. So this code indicates enemy troops are in the area. Not as bad as X-Ray.

Escort required. Bullets still flying and land at your own risk kinda stuff. I am confident that whatever problems the enemy may cause, I can handle it. If I had to call a medevac back in Surkay Tangay, I would probably call it an X-Ray. But not here, not now. *Don't make it sound worse than it is.*

"Line 7. Red Smoke." How will the pilots know the PZ (pick-up zone)? I have been carrying it all day; this is one of the reasons why.

"Line 8. 4 Charlie." A collective sigh of relief is being heaved across Afghanistan. Line 8 indicates the status of the patient, not his health. American or not. Military or not. Charlie means non-US. So for people who aren't familiar with the south, it could mean a NATO ally. But for everybody who is in the mentor business, it means Afghan. Not that anybody is happy about an ANP being wounded (except maybe some ANA). Rather, it means it wasn't an American. Not somebody we knew. Not someone whose stuff we will have to clear out. Whose family we will have to remember to visit when we go home. *Their country, their war. If someone has to catch it, better them than us.*

"Line 9. Open area, over." A description of the general area. Technically, this is only used for peacetime. In wartime, line 9 is supposed to indicate the NBC status: nuclear biological chemical. Back in the bad ole days of Ivan, the use of chemical weapons was assumed. So if it was nasty where we were, I would have to warn the pilots. But, thankfully, Afghanistan has been spared that particular misery since the Russians left in 1989. Landing won't be a problem. The 9-line is out. Time to wait.

"Copy all, Crazybear. Medevdac is twenty minutes from wheels up." Twenty minutes isn't bad. Plus ten minutes of flight time, give or take. Shouldn't change the equation on anybody. Time to get the PZ ready.

"You guys doing OK?" I enquire to Moore and Dhakal.

"Dhakal, good. How are the ANP?"

"One dead, four wounded. One bad."

"Fuck."

"Yeah, could be worse," Moore interjects. Yeah, it sure could. Could have been us. Could have been any of the three trucks in front of the truck that got it. Could have been a bigger bomb. Could have caused a gas tank explosion. Could have been anything. Hell, we could have missed it altogether and some poor jackass in a minivan could have hit it. In-shah-fucking-lah. Man get killed out here.

"Keep your eyes open. I don't think they are going to fuck with us, but you never know," I remind them. Twenty minutes minimum, thirty minutes probable till they show up. The clock is ticking again. I have to ration my time. First thing, check on the troops. I walk over to the other trucks. The ANP don't leave a driver or gunner; their trucks are stopped and empty. The ANP have walked about 500 meters in all directions and have of their own accord taken up good positions on the high ground. They are nonplused about the situation.

I walk over to the two American trucks. Same questions, same answers, same reminders. No one is stressed, just tired, a little bummed, and really pissed off. The feelings are the same. *We had these fuckers!* Today went right and now this fucks it all up.

Geno calls out, "How long to medevac?"

"Twenty minutes to wheels up, figure thirty to on the ground," I reply. He sounded a little bit on edge. Better check on how the wounded are doing.

I trot over to check things out. Things aren't going well. Ortiz has installed a cric tube in his throat. His face didn't look that bad, but I guess he wasn't breathing well. The procedure is technically called a cricothyroidotomy: an emergency tracheotomy where the medic cuts through the trachea in the throat and shoves a breathing tube in there. I ain't gonna do one, that's for sure. This guy has a tourniquet on each limb, an IV in him and is breathing through a tube Ortiz just cut into his throat. Oh, he is pretty awake and unhappy. He keeps moving his arms to try to take the cric tube out. I kneel down and grab his arms.

"Fahim, grab two ANP and have them help out Ortiz," I yell out. Fahim is closer. It looks like Siar is with Shah Khan, who is walking around checking his guys on the perimeter. Fahim spews some Pashto, and two of the closer ANP run over to help out. Each grabs an arm, and I stand back up. The guy just didn't look that bad, but I am not the medic.

"Ortiz, what do you need?" I ask.

"A fucking medevac!"

"Thirty minutes, it's all I got." He doesn't reply. His hands are full. The other wounded ANP look OK. Security is good enough. Time to clear the PZ.

Even though it is pretty flat and looks safe to land, I want to make sure. I need to make sure. What is a tragic inconvenience now will be a full-blown cluster fuck if something happens to the medevac birds. They are going to send two birds and both will probably land. I need to clear out about sixty by twenty yards of space where they can touch down. Everyone else has a job at this point, so I should do it. It is good to be useful. I start walking back and forth, slicing off about three meters each time, looking for sharp rocks that could mess up the tires, a branch that could shove through the floorboard, though I can see right off that isn't a problem. I am setting up the LZ about thirty meters to the west of the IED strike, farthest away from the hills. The slope is good, less than two percent. If the slope is too steep, the rotor blades can strike. I don't want to use the wadi, for reasons that are now obvious. Back and forth.

On my last pass, I see an old RPG round that failed to explode. "Oh, great! A fucking dud RPG round," I shout to no one in particular.

Gregory advises, "Just throw it out of the PZ!" There are few hard rules in combat, but many rules of thumb. Near the top of the list comes, "Don't make a bad situation worse." Looking down at the RPG round, I can tell it has been there a while. It is pretty weathered. The blowing sand has built up around one side. It's pretty lucky I saw it anyway. But still, let sleeping dogs lie. Leave dud RPG rounds the hell alone seems like the prudent course of action.

"I think I'll leave it be and set up a new PZ." I shout back.

"Scared?" he yells back.

"Damned straight!"

And with that I repeat the back and forth on the new PZ just south of the old one. As I walk back and forth, my anger is building. This isn't the first time I have been blown up in a wadi. But the last time I figured it was because we spent so long waiting to exfil. The 160th Special Operations Aviation Regiment "Night Stalkers" had provided the aviation support for a previous mission in Surkhagan. As their name implies, they fly at night. Well, the mission was done by noon, but we waited all day for night to fall (in May, that was until about 2300). That gave the Taliban a chance to put some IEDs on our probable routes home. I assumed that the IED was specially planted while I sat all day in the Surkhagan Valley. Today's mission was different. In and out; no screwing around. The wadis are used by everyone. I assumed that the Taliban wouldn't just put IEDs in wadis that could blow up any poor Pashtun driving by. I didn't pick this route, but I could have vetoed it and told the ANP to get out of the wadi. I am technically only advising the ANP, but who am I kidding? This was my mission. And now one guy is dead and another is pretty screwed up. He'll never dance the Afghan equivalent of the tango again, that's for sure.

Was it an IED for Duri the other night with Rob and Nomad? Maybe. So now the "perfect" mission isn't. Now it is messy and real, and the Taliban are getting the last—though muted—laugh.

I finish clearing the PZ. It looks good enough. At least no very noticeable RPG rounds or other obvious hazards. My real work is done. Double check the priorities. Security is still good. ANP are out to about a one-kilometer perimeter. Almost too big. But with the wide-open terrain, it is manageable. Two cops are picking up the pieces of green Ranger and the severed ANP. They found another body bag for him. I wasn't sure if we were out of them. Maybe they dumped a Taliban body. Wouldn't surprise me. A cop is 300 meters away, slowly rolling back the bent right front wheel. *Damn that went a long way.*

If a UAH had hit the IED, the whole crew might be dead. The light construction of the Ranger allowed the blast to go straight up instead of being transmitted through the solid body of an armored vehicle. *How is that for irony?* Total loss in armored vehicles is common. The police advisors in the south lost four US and a terp to a blast. How big? Who knows, exactly? Maybe bigger. Maybe a UAH would have survived. I am glad that question wasn't asked or answered today. Someday the bill will come due, however. All I can do is hope it isn't one of my guys when it happens.

I walk back to the casualty and see that he doesn't look good. Medevac better hurry. Time to double-check. I jog over to my HMMWV and check again with Zabul.

Ten minutes, they tell me, till wheels up. I check my watch. It has been twenty minutes already. They are running late. Might be bad. Nothing I can do. I walk back and see one of the casualties doesn't have an IV. He also doesn't appear to be too badly hurt, but he isn't moving much. His eyes are open and he is lying flat on his back.

I get closer and smile at him. He grimaces back. "Who assessed this casualty?" I shout out. Nobody answers. I repeat the question, asking Geno and Ortiz directly. Neither of them has. Since his clothes are still largely intact, and the two most knowledgeable medic types haven't done so, it seems like a good idea to make sure nothing else is wrong.

I go through the basic rundown: bleeding, breathing, bones, and treat for shock.

I first examine the outside of his uniform. There is some blood on the front, but not much. *His? Taliban's? Fellow ANP? Lunch from two weeks ago?* I don't know. I pop open my IFAK and grab my scissors. I glove up and then cut open his gray tunic. Over his right breast there is a small puncture wound. The guy is breathing fine, so I assume it is just a scratch, but it could be all the way through his lung. The bleeding is slight but still trickling out. Grabbing gauze, I clean it up and put an adhesive plastic seal over it, just in case it did puncture. After that, I roll him over and check for an exit wound. His back looks good.

The rest of his body appears to be clear of any more wounds. I firmly squeeze his extremities and torso, searching for obvious signs of broken bones. I shift his pelvis. The skeleton seems fine. Breathing is good. I look into his eyes. Pupils are good, small in the bright late afternoon sun. No obvious signs of concussion. I grab a nearby rock and prop his feet up on it. I have expended all my medical knowledge at this point.

"Geno, when you get a chance, check this guy out for me. He has one small puncture wound on his chest, but I don't think it penetrated the lung. I think he's OK, but you're better at this than I am. I'll help Ortiz."

"Roger." Geno and I exchange positions, and at this point there isn't much more we can do for Ortiz's patient. I hold up the IV bag and keep the guy from moving too much. He is in obvious pain.

"Can you give him something?" I ask Ortiz.

"Maybe, but I don't want to risk it," Ortiz replies

He still doesn't look that bad, but I think he was the TC, meaning he was sitting a foot away from a guy who literally got blown into pieces. Maybe it is all internal. *Hell if I know.* Sitting there, doing nothing, my thoughts start steaming again. *Everything was right. Less than ten klicks to Highway 1 and a damn near perfect mission.* The thought rolls over again and again in my head while I hold up the IV.

"Damn it, we were so fucking close!" I finally explode.

"Sir, it was still a good mission. Shit happens. Medevac is en route, PZ is secure, and we still got eight dead Taliban in the bag. Enemy gets a vote, too. You keep telling us that. Fucking relax already," Ortiz retorts.

He is stressed. His patient is in a hurt box. He is twenty years old and his job performance is assessed based on a whether a man lives or dies. He doesn't need the senior officer feeling bad for himself or being angry.

"Thanks. Sorry about that. Good job on the patient. Looks like he will make it." I attempt to be useful again. I can feel bad for myself later.

"He should, as long as his insides aren't too fucked up, and I can't tell that. What's up with medevac?"

"Should be in the air now. Any minute," I answer.

Less than thirty seconds later, I hear the call on my MBITR. "Any Crazybear element, this is Dustoff. We are two minutes out." Dustoff is the universal call sign for medevac helicopters. I am officially useful again.

"Roger, Dustoff, standing by."

"Roger, how are you marking the PZ?

"Red smoke. What is your approach?"

"North to south. We see your position now." At that, I hear the helicopters but still can't see them.

"Geno, how is that guy?" I ask Genovese, who was still checking the patient I had earlier.

"Fine! I'll get the IV, you get the birds down." Geno jogs over and I run to the southernmost point of the PZ I had cleared out. The helicopters do a south-to-north flyover and then turn around for their north-to-south approach.

I kick the dirt to determine what the winds are like and from what direction. Not bad enough to worry about. I pull out the smoke grenade and throw it twenty meters in front of me. Roughly the touch down point for the lead helicopter.

"We have your smoke" comes over the MBITR, and I raise my arms as I was taught in air assault school years before. The helicopters are bearing down on me but are a little low. I signal for them to come forward more, but they are having none of it. In a terrific cloud of dust, the lead bird touches down nearly on top of the RPG round I so carefully avoided. *Goddamn pilots.* The second bird lands behind it in an uncleared area.

Whatever.

The crew chief steps out and I jog out to meet him. We walk away from the bird to where we can hear over the unmuffled engines.

"Where is the urgent guy?" the crew chief asks. I point to him. "Load him last. Do you need stretchers?"

"No, we're good." Each vehicle keeps a stretcher on the back plus one that folds up in the trunk. All four wounded guys are on stretchers now. The crew chief walks over to one of the other wounded, and I direct Geno and Gregory to grab on. The four of us grab a handle and lift up the patient, who is surprisingly light. I walk straight to the lead bird but then the crew chief backs up and we move toward the second bird and push the stretcher in. The flight medics arrange the litter while we run back and get the next guy.

The process is repeated. Ortiz stays with the most seriously wounded until he is pushed onto the lead aircraft. As the four of us move back to the trucks in the familiar hunched posture, we expect the medevacs to lift off instantly. Instead, they just sit there. The PZ is safe, so I figure they are just making sure everybody is strapped down right. Still, they are big freakin' targets just sitting in the open plain. Putting too much trust in my

ANPs' security posture, in my opinion. Finally, in a cloud of dust they apply the power and adjust the pitch of the blades, soaring off toward FOB Lagman and Role 2.

The medic system is coded according to NATO standard. Role 1 is filled by Ortiz, the local medic. Role 2 goes to the first doctors that see the patients at the brigade level. Stabilize and keep them alive a little while longer. Role 3 goes to medical personnel back at KAF who can provide a lot of great treatment. Role 3 is a multinational medical unit—mostly Canadian—and can do damn near everything. Then it's Role 4 at Walter Reed in the United States or Landstuhl Regional Army Medical Center back in Germany. If they make it to Role 2, they generally live. The guy was alive and kicking as we put him on the bird, so he should be OK.

It is quiet and calm now. No more wounded to treat. The deafening noise of the helicopters is now a faint buzz in the background, soon to be inaudible. I motion to Siar to come over.

"Find Shah Khan; we need to get the hell out of here," I order.

The ground is littered with torn uniforms and used medical supplies.

"Ortiz, grab all the trash and uniforms and throw them on the wreckage of the truck. I don't want the Taliban dancing around with bloody ANP uniforms on Al Jazeera tonight."

Waiting for Shah Khan, I start grabbing the trash and moving it over. The Afghans have started copying me and are grabbing the pieces of the truck and everything else. The wreckage will be burned in place—no sense leaving everything else strewn about. The three dead Taliban in the back of the truck remain on the ground behind the wreckage. We are going to have to do something about that. It looks like all the weapons and gear have been taken out, though. The motorcycles are gone, too. They sure aren't going to leave those behind.

Shah Khan walks up with Siar, who says, "Sir, we have a problem."

No kidding, I think to myself. "What's up?"

"The ANP found another IED."

You gotta be fucking kidding, I think again. Surprisingly restrained, I limit my verbal reply to, "Great."

9

CROSSING THE RIVER

1845.

I walk with Shah Khan, Siar, and the good Samaritan ANP over to where he thought he saw the IED. Since the possible bomb is in the wadi, we stay out of the wadi and walk along the side. A standard pressure plate is built with springs strong enough in theory not to explode under a man's weight, but a vehicle will set it off. But as with many things homemade, we don't have Underwriters Laboratories here to be sure, so I intend to stay as far away as possible.

I have to tip my hat to the policeman for his due diligence. The site is a good 400 meters away from where we hit the IED. We finally get there, having worked up a good sweat. The ANP points at a spot that looks exactly like every other part of the wadi. I can't see a damn thing. The ANP is sure and I don't feel like taking chances, so we carefully walk over to the area and mark it with a couple of rocks and a piece of paper so we can find it again. Then we walk back and find Gregory.

"Grab a pop and drop. I don't think there is anything there, but we should make sure," I tell him.

"I've got some shock tube, can we use that instead?"

"Sure."

A pop and drop is a pre-prepared demolition charge comprising one block of C-4 plastic explosive (1.25 pounds), a blasting cap, detonation cord, a time fuse (black powder-soaked string encased in plastic to make it waterproof), and a fuse igniter. The fuse igniter is just a fancy, but dependable, lighter that uses an ammunition primer to start the time fuse. It is a plastic tube with a pull ring on one end that strongly resembles the pin on a hand grenade. It takes about five minutes to make one of these doodads, but Swampfox keeps one or two pre-made just for situations like this. The det cord is optional, as you can directly insert the blasting cap into the C-4. Generally, the blasting cap sets off the detonation cord, which has a knot of the stuff embedded into the explosive.

While everybody continues to stand around waiting, we trot back to the suspected IED site. Gregory lays out the demo charge and tapes the shock tube blasting cap to the tail of det cord hanging out of the block of C-4. A shock tube is a plastic tube lined with a tiny amount of explosives—you set off the explosives on one end and the explosion travels the length of the tube nearly instantaneously.

After ensuring no ANP are too close, Gregory starts to put the shock tube into the fuse igniter. "What the fuck? It doesn't fit," Gregory informs me. I look down and see that the observation is correct. The shock tube is smaller in diameter than det cord. The fuse igniters come with adapters to fit both as needed.

"Where the hell is the adapter?" I ask him.

"The what?"

"The adapter; the little green plug that goes in the end?"

"Oh, I dropped it."

The two of us comb the desert floor looking for the adapter while forty people stand around waiting for us. Eventually we find it and successfully prepare the shock tube.

"Fire in the hole!" Gregory yells and pulls the fuse igniter. There is a two-second delay (give or take) between pulling the fuse igniter and the charge going off. Gregory, who's never worked with this kind of charge before, gives a perplexed look at its failure to ignite. I just smile. Then the boom is heard. Based upon the sound and the amount of dust thrown up, we both can tell there was no IED. Still, just one pound of C-4 is impressive.

"Well, better safe than sorry. Let's get the hell out of here."

I am positive I said just that thirty minutes ago.

The ANP and US soldiers have done a good job of cleaning up all the crap and debris and piling it on the wreckage of the ANP Ranger. I walk over to my HMMWV and pull out a red thermite grenade. This is a heat-producing munition that looks just like a smoke grenade. When ignited, it shoots off a very hot thermal jet that was originally designed to destroy metal equipment. Probably overkill to set off a puddle of diesel in the desert sands, but it should do the job. War is about overkill, after all.

"Hey, Sir, can I throw it?" Gregory asks.

"Knock yourself out," I answer while throwing the two-pound grenade to him.

He pulls the pin and throws it into the middle of the diesel puddle. Not much happens initially. The puddle starts to burn like a low campfire. Within a minute, however, the plastic of the vehicle is burning fairly well and most of rest is engulfed in flames. I pull out my camera so when the ANP requisition a new vehicle, the bean counters will know why.

Gregory steps up. "Hey, Sir, get a picture." Burning wreckage in the middle of Afghanistan. It makes for a good shot.

Now, finally, let's get the hell out of here. I call over Siar and Shah Khan. We are standing around when the flames reach the ammunition that was left in the truck. The pop of the rounds exploding and the familiar buzz of something flying by my head at great speed add both urgency and brevity to the conversation.

"Siar, tell him let's get the fuck out of here as quickly as possible, but stay out of the wadis and roads." Siar translates and Shah Khan nods his head. He doesn't reply but merely walks off and yells at his men to get in the trucks. "We are going to get hit by this cook-off ammo. Let's hope they didn't leave an RPG round in there," I tell Siar, and the two of us jog off toward Moore and Dhakal. Everyone else is already in the trucks. I am again the last one in. Before I can get the door shut, Shah Khan is leading the trucks out of the wadi and into the open desert. I slowly jot a BFT message summary of the past hour's events. Being off any trail or road makes the typing difficult.

We are now moving across the plains at a glacial pace. The ANP are dismounted as often as not to ensure that the trucks can get through the various irrigation ditches and natural terrain obstacles all over the place. Only ten kilometers to go. I am looking around, curious and, not surprisingly, wide awake.

Major Gray, the Nomad commander, has some good news on the BFT. The ANP found the Taliban that the Apaches engaged. Apparently, they bled out. *Sure they did.* At this point I don't care. The western group was almost certainly the bomb guys. Dead IED planters, however they died, make me happy. Gray and the Romanians, who have increased their aggressiveness since they lost their beloved captain to an IED strike, have linked up with the ANP who were on Highway 1 with two dead Taliban and one really screwed up motorcycle. That's the good news. But Gray says they're picking up Taliban chatter on the ICOMs indicating that they are planning to ambush my convoy and are planting IEDs.

Ordinarily, this would be blown off as hyperbole. Taliban are always saying crap on the radio about what they are going to do. "We are planting twenty IEDs right now. There are 400 Mujahideen planning to attack Qalat City tonight." Blah blah blah. But considering the day's events, maybe some more credence should be given to the claims.

As for the IED threat: *Hell, good luck with that.* I don't have the first clue which way we are going next, nor does Shah Khan. We are going completely cross-country and traveling only where the terrain allows us. That is, until we hit Rigg's Road. I'll worry about that fording point when we come to it, however. As for the ambush, having smacked them earlier in the day, if we can find any Taliban willing to fight on this side of Surkhagan, it will only be because they are fleeing someplace else. Considering the anger and motivation of both the US and ANP, the Taliban would be pretty foolish to try any more shit today. So let them try the ambush, and I'll worry about the IEDs when we get back on the road.

Cannata back at Task Force Zabul also has a message waiting: "ISR sees two civ with weapons on wreckage of ANP Ranger."

Holy shit! I have completely forgotten about the ISR. It is still overhead providing feed! *Revenge is mine,* sayeth the pissed off senior ground commander.

"Reaper?" I ask.

"Is it armed?" is the real question. UAVs (unmanned aerial vehicles) can be armed, but the Reaper carries more munitions and is guaranteed to have junk hanging off the wings. Sometimes preds (drones) are armed, sometimes they aren't.

"Roger." Greg assures me that it is armed.

"Hellfire." The one-word reply implies my desire for a Hellfire missile to be dropped right on top of their heads. Greg gets the point.

Nice. I can't bring the dead ANP back, but a little payback would feel good and give me something positive to take back to Sarjang. My spirits are lifted, so I share the news over the radio. The responding chatter is invariably of the "Fuck, yeah!" variety. So now, instead of dutifully looking out of my three-inch-thick window I stare at the BFT screen awaiting confirmation of revenge.

A minute passes. I start to get impatient.

"Status?" I ask simply.

"ISR needs eyes on to engage." *What? ISR is eyes on, damn it!* I grab the hand mic to the SATCOM.

"Zabul Base, Crazybear 6."

"Crazybear 6, Warrior 3." Cannata is on, not his underling.

I dispense with call sign formalities. "Nothing friendly in that AO. Senior ground commander authorizes strike."

"Roger, wait, out." Cannata will see what he can do. I am fuming. These fuckers are dancing on the grave of my dead soldiers (police, actually) and now some puke sitting in Bagram or Kandahar Airbase sipping a Green Beans mocha frappuccino quad shot no foam light doesn't feel like pushing a button. I want to, but don't mention any of this over the radio. A consistent stream of profanities slips past my lips in a whisper no one can hear.

The BFT blinks again. Cannata isn't bothering with the radio. "No weapons release without eyes on target. You have to turn around." My whispered profanities are instantly increased to a sustained, prolific roar. Even without pushing the button to talk on the internal head set, everyone in the UAH hears me. Not the first time I lost my temper today.

"Sir, what's up?" inquires Dhakal.

"They won't fucking engage unless we have eyes on!" I reply, volume muted since I am using the headset. For a man whose first language isn't English, Dhakal shows a similar fluency in profanity. Moore does the same. Even Siar gets in on it, though he asks the pertinent question first.

"Are we going to turn around?"

"No. They will piss out the minute we head back, we still won't kill them, and the time we waste is more opportunity for IEDs or an ambush." I thought through this beforehand. No matter what, we aren't going to get these guys. Taliban spotters are watching us now. They will radio back if we turn around and that is all there is to it. *All the times I have read about predator strikes against the wrong target and these shitbags get a pass.*

The decision is made, and the wave of anger has come and gone. I am still not safely back in the FOB and there are still bad guys out there. I deliberately take a few deep breaths and share the bad news on the net. The replies are predictable as are the requests to turn around. I am not in the mood to explain my decision again, so I end the chatter with, "Negative. We aren't turning around." The silence over the net doesn't hide the knowledge of the fury being directed toward both me and the unknown air force officer who is going to let our cops go unavenged. Neither of us has a responsibility to explain our decision, but I will later so as to impart the lesson. *Just another kick in the balls, and we still aren't even on Highway 1 yet.*

Dusk is quickly coming; maybe an hour to go. We reach the outskirts of Khele Malal and the infamous Riggs' Road. There aren't many places

to cross the Tarnak Wa Jaldak River in the best of times, but this is one of
them. Once we hit the IED, the Taliban probably guessed we were going
to cross here. The dense and lush orchards, narrow streets, and overlooking hills are a perfect place to ambush us. I still don't think it's going to
happen, but I'm taking no chances this close to home. I can see Nomad's
vehicles as blue squares on my BFT. I can hear them on the radio as well.
Four days ago in Duri, we got the frequencies screwed up and couldn't
communicate. We sent up flares in the dark to mark our position to avoid
any friendly fire. One digit was wrong in the frequency "smart book,"
and that shut everything down. At least we got that fixed.

As we reach the outskirts of town, I call for dismounts to get out. IEDs
concern me more than an ambush. On foot we can see any possible signs
better and then there is the simple equation that if fewer people are in the
vehicle, fewer can die from one IED. The simple math of Afghanistan is
still of value.

Two more kilometers of walking. The town itself, insulated from
Highway 1 by the Tarnak, is another beautiful town. The irrigation system is well established, the mud huts larger, the walls around the compounds taller with nicer gates. The upscale suburbs of Zabul. The kids are
out; that is a good sign. The heat of the day has passed and I can smell
the evening meal being prepared. We walk along. Most of our eyes on
the road (though we are the fifth vehicle passing through—fairly safe in
theory) but some of our eyes are on the people and the receding hilltops.
As we come through the main part of town, Dhakal throws some candy
to the kids on the side, which is a rare gesture. The town's "atmospherics"
are good—"atmospherics" is fancy talk for "overall feeling." If there's an
ambush coming, the villagers don't know about it.

The road we're following veers sharply to the right and plunges down
to the Tarnak. It is called Riggs' Road because a guy named Riggs almost
drove off of it during an earlier mission. He is reminded of it endlessly.
The road is certainly narrow and certainly risky, but Riggs did make it
through OK. Other than the required extraction of seat cushion following the episode, there were no problems.

As we walk down the road, there's a cascading stream that flows to
rejoin the Tarnak after being siphoned off to water the orchards. The
children play alongside it. The flowing water can be heard even over the
creaking of the UAH's suspension; the still-darkening sky gives the scene
a very peaceful feeling. Right now, although I'm awake, I feel serene. I
would like to go up, play catch with the kids, share some food with them

and rest my back among the trees. Freed of my body armor, I would fall asleep instantaneously. Much nicer than the FOB. While the sun still hits the higher portion of the hill to our right, we are walking in the shadows. *This is pleasant*, I think to myself.

Only 500 more meters to the Tarnak and another 1,500 meters to Highway 1. The whole way (minus the river itself) is perfect IED terrain. There is only one way up and one way down on the far side of the river. IEDs are most often on the highway and these choke points right next to it. Cannata's predecessor was killed, along with three other US soldiers, on just such a trail. We simply can't avoid them, and the Taliban know it. Yet at this time, that risk is far from my mind. I am committed, and the decision to take that route is already made. *Inshallah*. Right now, in the cool of the shadows and the late afternoon, with the sound of laughing children and splashing water, it wouldn't be a bad way to die. There are worse ways to go. Eleven people have already died today for sure. Probably another ten are dead or dying in the hills we left hours ago. Three of my men are wounded, one severely. That's a lot of carnage. That's a lot of grieving families and enraged brothers. This mission happened because of me. Had I not made the plan, gotten the resources, and then gone ahead and carried it out, twenty more people would still be alive to listen to falling water and laughing children.

One of the first things a soldier learns to do in war is to dehumanize the enemy. Gooks, Huns, Japs, injuns, ragheads. Those aren't humans, those are enemies. A soldier protects humans and kills enemies. Simple. But the time comes to peel back that onion and see the truth. Most men fight for the same reason I do. They just happened to be born in the wrong country. And for that, I kill them. Or at least try. As a young lieutenant in the early nineties, I would hear the stories of the Gulf War vets. Burying the Iraqi soldiers alive with bulldozers. Hosing the bombed and broken draftees with bullets fired from coaxial machine guns from behind feet of armor. That was effective war. We won, they lost. We killed more than they killed. But while our anger was directed at Saddam, our wrath was directed at those he terrorized most of all. No matter how much the US soldiers hated Saddam, it was more than likely those we killed hated him more.

How many Shia and Kurdish draftees were killed in March 1991? Probably more than the Sunnis from whom Saddam garnered his support. Certainly orders of magnitude more than the Tikritis, whose tribe was really the only one to benefit from Saddam's reign. That was difficult to wrap my head around. While many of my contemporaries envied those who were first bloodied in the Gulf, I never have. And while that war is held up as the culmination of the military art (and it was, in many regards), it certainly wasn't a warrior's war. It was the cold war culminating. For fifty years our army had prepared to take on the Soviet horde. That the weakened, ill-trained, and ill-equipped Iraqi army was to be the relief valve for fifty years of pent-up frustration and preparation was almost unfair. But another of the maxims of modern war is this: If you find yourself in a fair fight, you didn't plan properly. That certainly wasn't a fair fight. But was today any more fair to the enemy?

I can think back. How frustrated and frightened were the Taliban when the Apaches started firing at them? They could hide, but they knew we were coming. If they fled, the chain guns hanging off the nose of the untouchable Apaches would tear them up. Perhaps if they hid, the Apaches would miss them. It took a dozen of them falling to figure that out, though. It wasn't a fight, it was a slaughter, a harvest. The Apaches could kill, and their targets could do nothing but die or hide, praying the modern infrared sights would miss them. Was that a fair fight? Should it have been? Is planting IEDs any more cowardly? Well, at least the Apaches aren't random. Before the Apaches pulled the trigger, they ID'd them. The one guy who was walking the trail was almost assuredly Taliban. But he was smart enough to put his gun down and play it cool and hide under a farmer's load. Maybe he won't pick the gun up again?

But the guy I shot, he got first shot and missed. Guess he shouldn't have missed. He had his chance, and that's more than 99 percent of the fuckers out here. More to the point, he chose his path. These guys chose to be Taliban. They chose to pick up arms. They weren't forced, they wanted it. Why they wanted it, who knows? Family, money, improved social status? Religion is probably pretty far down the list, if I were to really get to the heart of it. Yet, I bet they all wanted to be martyrs if I asked them. Maybe not today, of course, but eventually. But a hell of a lot better than killing Iraqi draftees, that's for sure.

Fuck it. They wanted to die as martyrs, and I am just fine with setting it up. *Win-win.* These existential rambling thoughts are pushed aside as it is time to get back across the Tarnak. Riggs' Road is behind us and I climb back into the UAH. The Tarnak is wide here with a nice gravel bottom—good fording site. And if it isn't, well, the ANP are going to figure it out first. Our convoy quickly splashes through the meandering river and accelerates up the steep bank. No talking will be heard until we are on Highway 1. No conversation goes particularly well with possible impending death. Only one minute after driving out of the river, however, we pull off to the side, where Major Gray and several ANP trucks are on the side of the road. Despite now being on the most IED'd road in Afghanistan, I still feel as though we have made it to safety.

I jump out to talk to Gray. He outranks me by date of rank, which means he was promoted to major before me. But I am his boss, de facto. He only tested this once in a disagreement and the colonel backed me up. It was uncomfortable for both of us, but clarifying it helped immensely. Gray has a lot of time in his area and knows it well. If I had another company-grade officer to put in his job, I would, however. Both because of the rank inversion and because I think Gray has gotten timid. Gray has different feelings, of course. There is more art than science behind this nonsense. But the boss put me in charge, and that is what matters.

Right now, that is all behind us. When Gray had his fight at Duri Ridge with Rob, I didn't hesitate to drive out to Surkhagan (along the same wadi where we left a burning Ranger and a man's soul behind about an hour ago) to help. And he has sat on this road, ready to do the same, for the past three hours.

I get out of my HMMWV, walk over, and shake his hand with a hug from the left. It is good to see another US element and someone I can talk to as a peer. He tells me about linking up with the Checkpoint 13 cops (who ordinarily operate with Swampfox) and the Romanians (off the road for only the second time I can think of). Time is short, however, and we need to drop the bodies off at Lagman and get home and showered. I am exhausted, and the day is almost over.

Shah Khan walks over to Gray and me and talks to Siar. "Sir, Julani wants to see you in Khar Joy," Siar translates.

Damn it. Khar Joy is to the north and Qalat is to the south. It is only a few klicks north, however. Earlier, Julani was in Tarnak, which is a hundred klicks south and which is why he couldn't come on today's mission. I bet he is pissed he missed it. Besides, the trucks with the goodies are going to do what Julani says, so I'd better do it as well.

"All right, let's go."

I circle my hand over my head, which means in this case, "Mount up."

Moore inquires, "What's going on?" I explain that Julani is in Khar Joy and wants to us meet there.

"Day keeps getting longer."

"Yep. At least we are still breathing."

"Good point." The vehicles all swing around, as we were all pointing south in anticipation of hearth and home. There are about twenty vehicles now, counting the additional ANP, the Romanians, and Nomad. The Romanians, their duty done for the day, do not swing around but rather head straight back to Lagman. I can't blame them; we all want to do the exact same thing. The gaggle of vehicles heads north at a hundred kilometers per hour, about the max speed for the UAH. Everyone is in a hurry, and we are just following Shah Khan's lead.

Within a few minutes of driving past rolling hills and orchards, we are in Khar Joy. We have yet again left Qalat District and are now in Shah Joy District, where the bulk of my original unit from Alaska remains attached to the Afghan army kandak. They aren't here now, unfortunately. It is always nice to see the guys I trained and came from Alaska with.

When Rob's little problem in Duri Ridge happened, they responded as well. But the team, Viper, took three hours just to get the Afghan army ready to go. Viper and Nomad share the same base, FOB Bullard. The Afghan base is co-located, much as Apache is attached to Eagle. The district police HQ is only a hundred meters down the road. It's a very convenient arrangement and makes for effective mentoring. Yet Shah Joy is acknowledged Taliban territory. In five minutes, we can probably be in a firefight. Neither the Afghans nor the mentor team commanders want to challenge that, which can lead to frustration on my part. But I have to give credit to Major Gray and Nomad. If it weren't for them setting a night ambush (and getting ambushed in the process), today wouldn't have happened.

Julani has brought another fifty cops and about twelve more Rangers with him. I pull off and see him sitting with a local storekeeper, sipping on an original Red Bull. The Red Bulls come from Thailand and are similar to the kind marketed in Europe and the United States with two main differences: Thai Red Bull isn't carbonated and contains a nicotine extract. If you don't usually use tobacco, the Thai Red Bull will knock you on your butt and keep you buzzing for hours. Julani, always with cigarette in hand, drinks them almost incessantly.

I greet Julani in the Pashtun manner, despite his Tajik heritage. His wife is Pashtun and he has lived in southern Afghanistan most of his life. His smile is genuine and his manner relaxed. As is customary, we navigate around the niceties. Having spent many hours with him and been in firefights together, I know that discussions around family are expected and reciprocated. Family matters are not usually discussed between Afghans and non-Afghans, but I am getting there with Julani. The five minutes of mandatory chitchat quickly passes, and I really want to get the day over with.

"Your men fought well today, and I am sorry about the death of your policeman. He was by my side for most of the fighting," I finally tell him when the moment is right.

Now is not the time to discuss the problems. I will discuss the executed prisoner later, when I have time and the passions of the day have subsided. Siar is translating, but I talk to Julani and look at him. "*Inshallah.* In war there is death, and we killed more of them than they killed of us. Today was a good day. I have been told you fought well and led my men against the enemy," he replies, quite graciously. He probably knows everything that happened today and probably knows more about today's fight than I do. The cold glint in his eye tells nothing and everything at the same time. I would hate to play poker with the man.

"We all fought together. Shah Khan did well."

"Yes, he did. He has more to learn, as do we all." *Oh shit, Julani does know what happened! Did Siar tell him? Fuck it. He was going to find out eventually anyway.* I want to close this conversation down and go home. The hunger is getting overwhelming as is the desire for sleep.

"I would like to take the bodies to Lagman and check on your wounded now. Will you join me for dinner there?" I ask him.

"No, we must go to police headquarters first." *What?* I push back a little, and while the smile never fades, Julani is getting a little irked. The back and forth continues for a few times until Siar translates the final exchange.

"General Sarjang orders it, and my men will obey those orders." *Damn it, I pushed it too far.* Sarjang runs the show, I am there at his leisure. Sleep and rest will have to wait. Julani had to invoke his general's name and rank when I should have done as he asked as a friend and comrade. He will forgive me (of course he will, I control his fuel supply), but I have taken a very small step back. I hope he will blame it on the lack of sleep, as I will.

"Of course. My apologies. The general would not have asked had it not been important," I finally concede.

"No problem, my friend. It has been a long day," says Julani, absolving me. I suddenly realize that he has been awake longer than I have as he was already in Tarnak Wa Jaldak when I got to PHQ this morning.

Yet again a twirl of the arm and the still-expanding convoy heads toward Qalat City, thirty minutes away. Major Gray with his three UAHs and Shah Joy District police head north toward their base in the epony-mously named district capital. It is forty-five minutes for them.

Speeding south, I again find myself relaxing, despite being on a road where an IED explodes every three days, on average. The Shah Joy police have taken the brunt of the casualties—four killed and three times that number wounded in the past month. Yet they keep driving it every day, checking the culverts for IEDS and just being out as police should. Culverts are preferred for IED placement because the Taliban don't have to dig. Almost all the culverts (114 at latest count) are inspected every day in the morning by both the Afghan police and the Romanians. Clearly the most dangerous job in Afghanistan, or at least in Zabul. The road is lined with orchards and small villages, the names on the map rarely matching the names used by the Afghans. Moghulzi Kalay, Mohammad Hasan Kor, Omar Khel, Layru, Moladin. Half are abandoned skeletons. The orchards give my sense of safety a bit of a jolt, since the Taliban like to put the canister IEDs in the trees. The Afghans slow for nothing, however, and I am again simply along for the ride.

In twenty minutes, we are on the northern edge of Qalat City and passing the turn into Lagman. I have forgotten to tell the rest of the unit we aren't stopping.

"Hey, we just passed Lagman," Geno breaks over the net.

"Roger, we have to go to PHQ first. Julani and Sarjang are big on this for some reason."

"Roger," is the surprisingly subdued reply. Most likely from exhaus-tion, not discipline. Regardless, I will take it. We pass the stick market, which is literally that. The roofs of the mud huts use sticks with diameters of three inches or so as stringers and then line them with brush and mud. In the absence of any wood in the area that isn't dedicated to orchards, saplings are imported and young boys spend the day stripping the bark off of the saplings. To my left is the stockyard/used car lot. Here, people barter for livestock and vehicles. Nothing is there permanently; it is just the place to bring things and sell them. The open-air butcher shop still has a side of goat hanging. Alexander's citadel overlooks us to the right. *Someday,* I remind myself, *I need to go up there and check it out.*

Continuing on, the main market is on my left now. Various Chinese plastic goods and Pakistani rip-off motorcycles are for sale. The entire town is less than a kilometer within the city limits. One of the many mosques hangs off the side of the hill in the literal shadow of Alexander's citadel. Next to it sits a dilapidated and closed medical clinic. The children are all out playing in the nice and somewhat cool dusk.

Lots of people are out enjoying the temperature, it seems. We reach the traffic circle and the man in the large hat waves as he stops traffic for us. Traffic would have stopped anyway; Julani doesn't *do* stopping in his province. As we pass the roses again, I notice there are several more cops on the gate than usual. Through the archway and we are again back in police headquarters.

Just me and about 2,000 of my best friends. "Holy shit," I mumble inaudibly. I don't hear anyone else saying it, but I know they are all thinking it. *It is an absolute zoo.* We park our trucks far to the side and I doff my body armor and long gun. The M9 pistol goes in my waistband, however. With this many people, who knows what is up.

Geno and Gregory walk up to me.

"Guys, stay off to the side and out of the crowd till I figure out what the fuck is going on."

They echo a "roger" and I grab Siar. "Let's get this over with," I tell him.

Together we move toward the crowd and Sarjang.

10

MILES TO GO . . .

1930.

Pistol tucked into my waistband, I see Julani bee-lining toward me. He grabs my hand and we walk, hand in hand, over to Sarjang's headquarters. Lots of civilians are there, along with NDS security guys. And *everybody* is looking at me. As we pass through the crowds, I try to keep from looking nervous. A lot of these folks are new to me; many are looking pretty hard-core Pashtun, which is to say Taliban. Right now, I probably am not the Taliban's favorite guy. Suicide vest at police headquarters is a fairly common tactic. There have been two in RC south in the past year. This would be a perfect target. *Inshallah.* Nothing I can do now.

Finally, I see Sarjang holding court on his patio and sipping tea. He has obviously been waiting for me. He is surrounded by most of the major players in Zabul. "Motherfucker, Sir. Everybody is here," whispers Siar. *They sure are.* As we approach, the provincial chief of NDS, the deputy governor of the province, and a major from the ANA all rise to greet us. I greet them all in the Arabic *Salaam alaikum* individually and they reciprocate with handshakes. I greet Sarjang in the more familiar Pashtun manner. The major from the ANA looks Tajik, but the rest are Pashtun. The deputy governor and chief of NDS then greet me in the Pashtun manner. *That's new.* I've never been on such familiar terms with them. We end all the greetings with the traditional right hand over the heart with a slight bow. Sarjang hugs me and invites me to sit. The deputy governor moves aside, and I sit directly with Sarjang. Ordinarily, I sit in the background as Sarjang represents at the large councils. Today is different, obviously.

Siar is not as refined as Fahim at these higher echelon conversations. He is clearly uncomfortable but still enjoying his chance to be the interpreter at this level. I would have preferred Fahim in this audience. His language skills are a little stronger and he is clearly from a more educated and upper-class background. But Siar has earned the right to be here. *Let him enjoy it.*

The crowd, mingling and noisy, has grown noticeably quieter at this point. I wonder how long they've been waiting. Now I know why Julani was so insistent. Sarjang congratulates me on the mission. Shah Khan is standing by and I extend all honors to him. Sarjang smiles and nods his head. He knows what happened. *How?* I don't know, but he knows. He probably knows better than I do the overall picture of what has happened. Just like Julani. *Who mentors whom?* I wonder for the millionth time. The deputy governor then apologizes that the governor couldn't be here, but explains that he was in Kabul and he extends his thanks and congratulations for a mission well done. A provincial governor apologizing to an American major. *Strange times indeed.*

The NDS chief is giving me a strange smile. He, too, can be expected to know everything that happened. His knowledge, I suspect, comes from the Taliban side, however. I figure his smile is fake. He might very well be seething. The Apaches were able to destroy the Taliban largely because of the disinformation I used him to spread. I expected him to tell the Taliban that the Apaches won't shoot except in self-defense. Now at least a dozen are dead and the rest may well be blaming him. His life may be in danger because of today. At the very least, his credibility will take a hit. *Fuck him. Lie with dogs, you get fleas. If he wasn't in cahoots with the Taliban, then he has nothing to worry about. And if he was, well, that isn't my problem.*

The Afghans assume, correctly for the most part, that Americans can't see through the surface and that we are entirely too trusting. The NDS chief has played that assumption and now he got caught in it. Or maybe he didn't. They aren't lies if everyone knows you are lying. The problem is, Americans *don't* know it. We aren't attuned to it. And even the Afghans who are truly on our side have to deal with the politics and undercurrents long after we leave. It's a fascinating puzzle that would be more enjoyable if the results for failure weren't so deadly. Regardless, I lied to the NDS chief. He knows I lied. I know he knows. I used him to deadly effect, and his mastery over the Americans, which I know he enjoyed manipulating, has been nullified. *Today must have really sucked for him. Good.*

Despite the crowd obviously waiting for Sarjang and the provincial entourage, he still maintains Pashtun hospitality and the NDS chief, the deputy governor, and I talk for at least ten minutes, sipping tea and enjoying frosted almonds (which Sarjang himself doesn't like but usually puts out for me, since it's my favorite Afghan snack). Sarjang munches on roasted chickpeas (which I could never choke down) and the delicious white raisins.

The ANA major is silent and obviously angry. That the ANA major general only sent a major as a representative was a slap in the face to Sarjang. But I suspect Sarjang is even happier because it shows how angry the ANA are that the ANP had the successful mission. The dynamic of the whole situation is very funny. *Still so much to learn, and I leave in two months, just when I'm starting to get my rhythm.* The thought of extending flits across my mind again. Promises. I volunteered and promised my wife I wouldn't extend. She knew such thoughts would fill my brain. She was right, and no, I won't extend. The knowledge of the short amount of time remaining allows me to savor the moment that much more. Most of the conversation is among the Afghans; Siar only translates what is pertinent. It gives my brain a chance to relax and wind down. *Still so much to do today.*

After about fifteen minutes, Sarjang rises and the entourage moves toward the crowd. I can now see what the true delay was. All the bodies, weapons, and motorcycles have been offloaded from the trucks and arrayed in relatively neat lines. An L-shaped arrangement with the dead Taliban, removed from the body bags, arrayed in front of a table filled with captured weapons, whether from today's fight or not, I can't tell. A rusted-to-crap AMD-65 (the weapon issued to the ANP) makes me suspect this may be a way to unload some worthless guns and make the Taliban look bad.

And now I see all the cameras. *This is a press conference. Time to be scarce.* This is the other half of mentorship. No matter how much this was my operation, in the eyes of the world—and, more to the point, the Afghan people—this was an ANP mission from start to finish. Fine with me. I hang back and snap some pictures while the ANSF's Zabul security team representatives sit in solidarity, having collectively beaten back the enemies of Afghanistan. It looks pretty good.

At the table, Sarjang sits with the ANA major on his left and the deputy governor to his right. The NDS chief is on the other side of the deputy governor while next to him is a captain with the ANP who is always around and says nothing. He is important, but I still haven't figured out why. Julani, surprisingly, is nowhere to be seen, neither is anybody who was with me today. Shah Khan, the nominal commander of the mission, is the only one present. Ironically, many of the police standing behind the row of dignitaries have on body armor and turbans, indicating they are fresh from the field where they are palace guard. *Pretty funny, I guess.*

I watch the proceedings for a while and go hunting for Mahmoud to thank him and see how he is doing. I find him joking with the guys from Swampfox, far from the cameras. He is in a good mood. While Mahmoud is out of sight, Shah Khan enjoys his place directly behind Sarjang. Today was very good for Shah Khan. He made Sarjang look good, and that is going to take him a long way. Good on him, almost everybody got what they wanted today. Except the Taliban and one very unfortunate ANP.

The motorcycles are lined up with the burnt-out hulk on one end and the nicer ones toward the table. My personal booty for the day is one functioning motorcycle and the hulk. I still have plans. The guns on the table are jingled. "Jingle" is the all-encompassing adjective for items decorated in the Afghan way. The term originates from the practice of decorating trucks all over with complex, paisley-like paintings and lining the bumpers with dangling metal trinkets. As they bounce down the road, they make a not-unpleasant jingle. So the trucks are known as "jingle trucks." Things that come from jingle trucks (which borders on everything, in this landlocked country that lacks a functional railroad or thriving industry) are jingly. So jingle radios or—in the British permutation of the term—jingly radios. Once back in KAF, I heard the thick Cockney (to my untrained ear anyway) griping of "jingly fags." Afghan cigarettes in normal American.

When it comes to weapons, the Afghans usually paint them and wrap them with what appears to be bright plastic bicycle handlebar tape. The RPG on the table has some spangles glued onto it. The PKM's bipod is wrapped in bright green tape while a pink sticker is on the feed tray cover on top. The stock of the AK is similarly wrapped, though with red tape. They certainly are a decorative people. The landscape can be subdued, but when given the choice, the Afghans go for color. This is true for both Taliban and ANSF. It's very common to see men in bright pink or light shades of purple. More true to nature; it is the male of the species who is most resplendent in his natural colors, at least in Afghanistan. Perhaps it's the rest of the world that has ignored nature and only the Pashtun male has remained true. Regardless, gender-based color association has no bearing in this most masculine of societies. One of many ironies.

My eye is drawn to the ten dead bodies aligned neatly in front of the table. The faces show the rigor mortis as do some of the limbs. The somewhat early onset can be blamed on the physical exertion they were engaged in at the time of death. Running for their lives. They are filthy, as only dead Taliban can be. They are all skinny and none looks to be older than thirty. Only one has shoes on—cheaply made dress shoes with the back of the shoe stomped down to create an ad hoc slipper. Did the rest fall off? Were they taken off? If so, by whom? By the ANP? Fleeing Taliban who were still alive? The man himself in a last, unfathomable act? A certain pity suddenly overwhelms me and, like my anger, passes. These guys really didn't have a chance. But that is the whole point, isn't it? The Pakistani ID card sitting as a prized trophy on the table of trophies mutes my pity to a certain degree. At least one of them made a very deliberate, and stupid, decision to come to a country he wasn't invited to.

There is little blood, even from those with horrific injuries. Because they are lying on top of the body bags, the blood has pooled below them unseen and soaked into their clothing. One body bag clearly has a leak, however. A blood trail flows down from the bag along the slight slope in the rocky dirt. They should show these ten dead Taliban to the school-children in Pakistan. This is the truth of Jihad. No glorious funerals, no weeping but proud mother. Lined up like ducks after a hunting trip to be thrown about as so much garbage, useful only as proof of victory. And yet further indignities await them.

The sun, so long hanging in the afternoon sky, finally falls out of sight behind the ridge just south of Alexander's citadel. The call to prayer goes out from the mosque, only meters from the macabre festival I am witness to. And that ends the press conference. Sarjang, a fairly religious man, seeks me out first prior to praying. It takes me a few moments to get Fahim over. Siar is busy talking with Shah Khan.

"It is time to pray. What do you need from me?" Sarjang asks.

"Sir, I need the bodies loaded onto a Ranger to be taken to Lagman. They can be reclaimed tomorrow morning, but we need to put them into the computer. Also, I want one functional motorcycle and the destroyed one. I will check on your wounded at Lagman while I am there," I reply. Fahim quickly translates for me.

Sarjang's reply through Fahim is encouraging. Three of the wounded have already returned to PHQ and are resting now.

"Wonderful news. I will see you tomorrow. *Dai Chodadi Pa'aman.*"

"*Dai Chodadi Pa'aman.*" A warm handshake with the left arm over my right shoulder and Sarjang moves to the mosque. How he will address to-day's activities with Allah is a mystery known only to him. Julani suddenly appears at my shoulder. He points to where the bodies have been loaded onto a single Ranger, whose suspension sags heavily at the weight. I hope they don't fall off while driving through Qalat City. That would be awkward. He smiles as my functioning motorcycle is brought over. It is carefully loaded onto the back of the UAH between the hatch and tire while the destroyed one is similarly loaded onto Geno's HMMWV. *Thank God these guys don't ride Harleys.* Julani, it would appear, will accompany me to Lagman. *All right with me.*

Another sweep of the arm and the men of Swampfox slowly don their gear. Everybody is dragging ass right now. *And miles to go before I sleep.* Frost's poem echoes in my head. Everybody wants to interpret it, but for a traveler maybe it is nothing more than what is stated. A desire to just lay my head down and rest in the first comfortable spot I find. The little impatient horse finds its place with the soldiers of Swampfox. They want to go home now. But not yet.

I get my crap on as the timeless dusk moves to very dark in only minutes. It has been maybe fifteen minutes since the sun finally set, but headlights are already required. I switch the radio frequency to Zabul Base. This close we don't need the SATCOM. Since it is a private net, I can speak on it freely without fear of trampling over more important conversations.

"Zabul Base, Crazybear 6."

"Go ahead, Crazybear."

"En route to your location. Have bodies to be received and HIIDEd. Where do you want me to drop them off?"

"Wait, out."

No problem, we can still drive there and get the answer on the way.

Moore and Dhakal express their readiness in softened voices. Dhakal has been standing in body armor comprising half again his weight for a good fourteen hours today, nearly immobile. Moore has been crammed behind a HMMWV steering wheel for the same time, knees jammed high enough to brush the wheel. Neither is complaining. Sometimes I just have to love soldiers.

"Almost done, guys," I assure them.

The three VICs call out their REDCON 1s and we roll in the wonderfully cool and surprisingly dark evening.

"Feels nice up here, Sir," Dhakal observes.

Back along the way we came earlier, the shrunken convoy passes the now-abandoned traffic circle. Once over a bridge crossing a wadi leading to the Tarnak, we take the left turn toward Lagman. The dirt road is worn hard and relatively smooth by the incessant heavy traffic. A holding area for jingle trucks is on my right as we approach the gate manned by Romanian soldiers. The jammers are again switched off as the improvised gate is moved aside.

The Romanians are still largely equipped with Soviet-made equipment. One such vehicle is the BRDM (pronounced bur-dum). This is a much larger cousin to the armored HMMWV. It has four wheels, but it's shaped more like the armored personnel carriers of the Cold War era than the SUV shapes of the modern UAH. The Romanians have figured, correctly, that it would be more difficult to push through a twelve-ton armored vehicle than a metal bar across the road. So a BRDM sits across the entrance to Lagman and they drive it back and forth as a movable gate. Effective, if inefficient.

As our vehicles file past, lots of smiles and waves from the Romanians. While often the target of the Taliban IEDs, they rarely get a chance for payback.

"This one's for you guys," I would like to say.

Immediately past the front gate there is a HMMWV ambulance and a soldier waving us over. Moore pulls up and rolls his window back. Apparently, they want the bodies dropped off right here. No problem; I have been looking forward to it all day.

HIIDing a dead man is a dirty, depressing, and unenjoyable task. It takes twenty minutes to HIIDE a live, cooperative subject. It takes about twice as long for a dead one—longer, if rigor mortis has set in. At the operations meeting only a few days ago at Lagman, I mentioned the HIIDing of the bodies recovered from Rob's TIC at Duri Ridge. One of the intel fobbits at Lagman complained, half jokingly, that he never gets to HIIDE dead Taliban. I promised him that the next time we had a dead Taliban, I would bring him to Lagman so he would have his chance. I now see that same soldier standing by the ambulance, HIIDE in hand, eagerly awaiting his sought-after opportunity. I can also see that nobody told them how many bodies because his eyes widened and his jaw dropped slightly as the ANP Ranger full of bodies pulled up.

Chuckling to myself, I step out to watch the hilarity ensue. "Is this where you want the bodies?" I innocently inquire.

"Yeah, but—wait, how many are there?" the hapless guy asks.

"Ten. Siar, tell Julani to unload them here. The ANP will pick the bodies back up tomorrow. Later," I say as I walk back to the HMMWV.

Moore and Dhakal are laughing. I had told them the story earlier. Now it is time to say thanks to the aviators, who made this all possible.

"Alright, let's get to Corsair," I call over Swampfox's net. Corsair is the call sign of the aviation unit from the 82nd Airborne Division. It's only another hundred meters up the road into Lagman. Lagman is the older and slightly more chaotic cousin to Apache. It started off small and has grown in an unplanned and ad hoc fashion for the past seven or so years. The Special Forces compound is to our right, with its own walls and Afghan security force. It also has its own, and much better stocked, chow hall. Being a major and having done a few missions with them, I arrogantly go in there occasionally to grab a snack or eat with the major in command of the SF in Zabul, who's a guardsman and full-time police officer. He is the only one who doesn't grow a beard in the SF community in Zabul. The Corsair area was just dirt three months ago. More ad hoc growth. The Romanians have their own slice, along with the Americans from Germany. It is old, dirty, disorganized, and a lot more laid back than Apache. It is also where Swampfox and the PMT need to be. Apache is really just for the ANA. Why Swampfox got lumped into there, I still haven't figured out. But it was a bad call.

We pull up to aviation land and again we all remove our body armor. "Alright, take off the motorcycles. I am going to go find the commander," I order Gregory. Everyone is taking off their gear. Lagman has a good chow hall and everybody is hungry as hell.

"Sir, I am going to rotate the guys through chow." Geno tells me.

"Good call," I agree over my shoulder as I walk into the tent serving as the TOC for Task Force (TF) Corsair. To my right as I enter is Maj. Dave Bresser. One year behind me at West Point and a fellow swimmer there. He was team captain the year after I left. He is now the executive officer of the aviation TF. The greeting is enthusiastic and warm. I have largely worked through him to get what we needed today and he delivered as promised. "Hey, is your boss around? Got something for you guys. Could you grab the Apache guys, too?" I ask. Turns out his commander, a female lieutenant colonel, is in the other side of the TOC. "Hey, Ma'am, brought you a gift. It's outside," I inform her. We all walk out toward the HMMWVs and Dave finds the Apache pilots—one woman and three men. Theirs were the voices I heard earlier today. I thank them all, and then immediately ask them the burning question of the day.

"What in the hell is your call sign?"

"What do you mean?" one of the warrant officers asks.

"It sounded like you guys were saying 'Repair,' like repair a truck. But that is lame as hell. So I figured it was 'Reaper' or something like that." At that they all laugh and explain that they asked for Reaper when they came into theater, but someone already had it, so they were given Repair. At least I wasn't losing my hearing or my sanity.

As we walk up with the pilots, they get a confused look at the scorched motorcycle. Then I explain this was the motorcycle they lit up and they saw flaming from FLIRs. Now the smiles break out and they understand. Pilots rarely get the souvenirs that the ground pounders get. I figure they earned this trophy. A forgotten wit once observed, "The French fight for honor, the English fight for glory, and the Americans fight for souvenirs." A good souvenir proves you aren't a fobbit. While most of Swampfox and the teams out and about have claimed some type of proof of non-fobbithood, it's tougher for the pilots. They should, if all goes well, never step foot outside the FOB. God help the pilot who lands just to pick up a trinket as proof of being "in action." The Apaches were the only reason today happened, and I fully intend to show my thanks and stay in their good graces. I had hoped this offering would cover that. It turns out it does.

"I know just the place," the commander declares as two pilots heft the recognizable hunk of blackened metal and follow her. What the hell. Most of the guys who aren't at the Lagman chow hall follow, too.

Befitting an established unit with a real patch and flag and actual history, this battalion from the 82nd Airborne Division has erected a flagpole with a unit identifier and a little stone marker. It's the centerpiece of their corner of Lagman. The burned-out trophy is placed center stage, directly in front of the flagpole. *Not bad. Maybe they are just humoring me, since it was a pain in the butt dragging that thing back. But still. Relationship building.* I am reminded yet again that, for all my rank and freedom, I actually control damn little and I won't get shit done if I don't play the game. This is about as honored as a burned-out hulk can possibly get.

I again exchange thanks with the aviators, but there's more to do and the night is growing longer by the minute. Now on to step two of the triumph: showing off.

I walk over to the HMMWVs and find the operational motorcycle I demanded. Moore helps me lift it down from the back of the HMMWV. The key is still in the ignition. Twelve hours ago some Taliban was puttin' away on this thing, scurrying to the safety of the hills east of Surkhagan. Now he is dead—or at least walking—and I am going to ride his motorcycle over to Lagman. Maybe give it to Cannata. *Who knows?*

Clutch in, first kick starts it up. I work the gears all the way up to put it in first and let out the clutch while goosing the throttle. The engine whines impotently. *The thing isn't in gear. What the hell.* I am not a motorcycle rider, but I learned over at Apache on some captured Chinese dirt bikes. But this is my first time on the Yonda. I put it in neutral, pressing down on the shift lever with my foot, and let the clutch out. The bike lurches forward and stalls. OK, like everything else here, this jingle bike is a little weird, but I think I have it figured out now. Amid the guffaws of my soldiers watching me fiddle around, I get the bike moving. As I enjoy the breeze on my face, I can envision how nice it would be to putt around the desert on one of these, assuming UAVs and Apaches aren't waiting to kill me.

The aviation compound and SF compound expand past the original boundaries of the FOB, so I have to go around the old Hesco wall. This route brings me to the aid station. I see Ortiz and Geno walking in, so I park the bike and join them. I walk in to the Role 2. Since the place is cleaned out except for one soldier on duty, it takes a while to get the point across and ask what happened to the severely wounded ANP. I assume he was flown on to KAF and Role 3. No, the female medic informs me. Three released and the KIA. *Huh?* There were four wounded and one KIA, and the KIA was with me. No, one KIA on the bird and three wounded. All three of us figure it out at the same time. I thought Ortiz would be pretty shaken up, but he is nonchalant about it. He explains that the ANP was more severely injured internally than I could tell just by my few glances and that he had been concerned he wasn't going to make it. Ortiz was prepared for the news; I wasn't. Yet another of today's ups and downs.

Again, I have the gut-punched feeling. *Get them alive on the bird and they will live* has been a reassuring thought my whole tour. We got him on the bird alive. I saw him moving, eyes alert as we loaded him on. *Damn it! Inshallah.* What else can someone say at this point?

Deflated, I walk into Zabul's TOC next to the aid station to say "hi" to Cannata. My own TOC is half a tent and a BFT in a corner with a couple of computers on desks made of two-by-fours and plywood, a couple of maps on the wall, and a little TV with a built-in DVD player. A coffeemaker completes the picture. No TOC is complete without a coffeemaker. My TOC is a half-assed little thing.

In Zabul's TOC, there are two rows of tables with about eight chairs behind each one. They all face a wall lined with a couple of plasma screens showing the BFT display and the surveillance cameras around Lagman, split-screened. Behind the two main rows is a raised chair on which sits the "battle captain." He is the ranking guy making the decisions when the commander isn't around, which is usually. In the other chairs are mostly US with a couple of Romanians. They pull twelve-hour shifts, seven days a week. These are the guys who got our medevac today. They also got our Apaches and were the go-between on the ISR assets. This is a place that looks the part, unlike so many other places in Afghanistan. I give a heartfelt "Thanks!" to the guys in there for all their help. A few replies of "Good job!" come back.

Captain Cunningham, the battle captain and Cannata's righthand man, is there but Cannata isn't. Cunningham is your typical young staff captain. Waiting his turn at command, doing the heavy lifting of staff work. The bench. Except that even the bench has a part to play. His technical title is the "Chops." Current operations. It's a good job, especially deployed. If you can't be a commander, Chops is as good as it gets. He was probably the primary guy on the other side of the BFT today. He's a pretty funny guy and keeps a running list of humorous things heard in and about Zabul. They are fun to read and it's always interesting at meetings watching him and waiting for a comment to make the list. I talk for a few minutes and give him my personal thanks. I ask where Cannata is. He is at a meeting. How long? Going to take a while. *Whatever. Screw it.* With another dead ANP on my mind, I don't feel much like gloating and high-fiving anymore, anyway.

I tell Cunningham I will catch him later and go to grab something to eat. Walking alone, I go through the screened doors. The chow hall here stays open pretty late, so they still have some food out. Signing my name on the sheet, I realize I'm not nearly as hungry as I thought I would be or should be. The gut punch is still there, draining my appetite. A motley mix of civilians are there serving the food. I grab a plate full of indeterminate meat and move to the drink dispenser. A Coke and a dessert (the desserts from KBR are awesome) fill out the post-battle meal. Then a glance around for a place to sit. Maybe Cannata is here or someone else I know. In this chow hall, probably 200 can sit at a given time. Apache's can fit sixty.

I see a couple of Swampfox guys and grab a seat near them, but not next to them. I still am not, and will never be, part of their team, according to both history and position. Command comes with a price. While they are laughing and joking, I hover near the periphery of the conversation. They seem to have no problems with how the day went. All the US made it home and lots of dead bad guys. It is all relative, I guess. I am still reliving the failures in my head. Two dead ANP. Failing to get weapons release for the guys dancing on top of the burned Ranger. Failing to anchor the Taliban in the hills of Surkay Tangay. Failing to keep the prisoner safe. Is it reasonable to expect nothing to go wrong? No. But I should always try my best to make it perfect. Maybe I'll get there someday. Even if I do, what can I really change?

Never take a wadi when I can go cross-country. No matter how long it takes. Make sure any future prisoners are guarded by a US soldier. Index my targets. *OK. Major problems solved.* A proactive plan lifts my spirits a little and allows me to focus on the positives. And there were quite a few. Most of them are stacked by the front gate. With that, I move on to the meal at hand and finish it quickly. It appears I am the last one from today to eat. Everyone else is done.

"All right, guys, let's go home." I look longingly at the large coffee dispenser, but hopefully I will be asleep soon and coffee might work against that.

My motorcycle is still parked near the aid station. Replacing the key, I start it up and putt back to where the vehicles are waiting. As the wonderfully cool air passes over my face, my mind goes through today's remaining tasks. I desperately want to avoid the paperwork and emails until tomorrow. I know with certainty, however, I cannot. I have to wait till the team is done showering before I can scrub the blood and dust off my body, regardless. I might as well make good use of the time. The simple reports don't take long to complete. They likewise are effectively worthless for disseminating useful information besides casualty counts, which remain the only metric that anyone cares about. After I clean my body, I will clean my weapons and gear and complete the final task that, if I thought about it, anyone will ever care about. *Almost home.*

Guys are sitting on top of the hoods of their UAHs or lying on the back hatches. Many are smoking. The conversation is muted but light-hearted. They, too, sense that today was a little different. Today will be a day most of them remember for the rest of their lives. Days like that are rare in life. Maybe less rare in Zabul.

I check with Geno to make sure that everyone is there and that everybody has eaten. A quick count confirms that we are ready. Siar helps me hoist the motorcycle into the back of the HMMWV, securely wedged between the spare tire and trunk lid. Everyone is slower yet to re-don their gear, me included. We aren't home yet, so one last thing before we go home.

"Bring it in real quick!" I shout out. I need to make sure everyone has his head on straight.

"First off, this will be short. Good job today to everyone. I know a lot of shit happened and emotions were high. You all did amazingly well. I am proud to have been with you guys today. For those who don't know, one of the wounded ANP died. Ortiz, you did a great job on him and I am sure there isn't a medic out there that could have done better." I hear a few of the men utter "Good job!" and slap each other on the back. Ortiz keeps his head down.

"We aren't home yet. Two more miles and we are done. We have pissed off a lot of Taliban today and they are going to want payback. I don't think they have the balls to try it tonight, but don't take any chances. We are all tired and want to get back. But let's get back safe. Gunners, drivers stay alert. TCs stay awake. Let's finish this off right. Hooah?"

I hear a few subdued cries of "Roger!" and "Hooah!" as the gathering breaks up. Just like they did in the morning, sixteen or so hours ago, the gunners lower themselves into the hatches. Dahkal goes up through the inside of the HMMWV. Moore hands him the restraining strap and puts on his own helmet and then his headphones. Quick checks within the vehicle confirm we can talk to each other. Siar looks ready to fall asleep. The BFT screen is blinking urgently with unread messages. They can wait. I get on the net and inform Zabul base we are heading out.

"VIC 1, REDCON 1," comes on the radio. I am going to run in the middle as number two.

"Everybody good?" Siar, Dhakal and Moore all reply they are good.

"VIC 2, REDCON 1," I say over the radio.

"VIC 3, REDCON 1."

Geno's truck moves out as soon as the last call is complete. Down the road toward the gate. The Romanian soldiers wave as the BRDM backs away, releasing our three vehicles into the perfectly clear Afghanistan night.

11

THE FINAL MISSION

2350.

Satellite phone in hand, I sit down on the concrete basketball court next to the bunker we used at the start of the day twenty hours earlier and power on the phone. After I enter the code, it takes the phone a few minutes to find the satellites and I take a moment to stare into the gorgeously clear night sky. I grew up in the desert and I vaguely remember skies like this. The Milky Way, forgotten by most of urban America, stretches across the sky. The planets are brilliantly visible. I thank my luck that the moon has not risen yet, so the stars are undimmed in their outstanding display. It is breathtaking and serene and helps to calm me before the call goes through.

Phone calls are tough. When I was serving in Bosnia, we soldiers got one brief call home a week, ensuring that conversations were positive and mostly about missing each other. But now I can call several times a week, either in the morning or in the evening. The regularity of the calls allows the regularity of home life to slip into this life. This shifting between lives is stressful. It magnifies the grotesque nature of combat when juxtaposed to hockey game play-by-plays or diaper-changing stories. I can't tell my wife all that I see, and I have to edit on the fly and judge what she can accept and what she can't. Each child, of varying degrees of maturity and language skills, must similarly be talked to in a precise manner that shifts each day, depending on what happened to them and what happened to me. The only advantage I have today is that I can beg to shorten the phone call due to the late night and my desperate need for sleep.

I punch in the numbers and in seconds hear my wife's voice, literally on the other side of the world. *Ain't technology great?*

"Hey, you," she answers. She knows based upon time of day and caller ID that I am on the other end.

"Hey, you," I say. It's the basic reply. Phone calls home must follow the expected protocol so as not to raise alarm.

"What's the matter?" she asks. Apparently, I have slipped up in only two words. *Let's see if I can play it off.*

"Nothing, just tired, long day." *That should work.*

"No, that's not it. What happened?" *Damn, she is good. Miss Cleo ain't got shit on my wife.*

"Big day. You might read about it tomorrow," I fess up.

"Anybody get hurt?" She cuts to the chase.

"Two police got killed, all the US are OK." I bypass the Taliban. It is not who she is asking about and she really couldn't care less.

"Are you OK?" She knows I am not hurt, but she also knows that dead police hang on my conscience every time.

"Yeah. Really just tired." "OK" is a good enough definition for how I feel, I guess.

"You want to talk about it?" I would love to talk about it. I would love nothing more than to sit down with her and talk for hours or days about what today was like and how I felt. The joy, fear, anger, satisfaction, frustration, disgust, embarrassment, exaltation, exhaustion, and every other conceivable emotion cycling through my mind and body throughout the day in varying degrees and combinations. But certainly not tonight and most probably never. Not with her; not with anyone. I am not sure anyone can speak about such things fully. All the power of life and death and I am powerless to express fully what today was to me. To her, I can admit some of the emotions, but not the ones that can't be understood unless you have been in combat. To the combat vets I can express some but not completely leave myself exposed and vulnerable as a full confession would. In various combinations I will tell the story of today, of my year in Afghanistan, of the piece of myself I gave willingly to a people and country who neither want nor appreciate my contribution. Most of whom would, in all actuality, rejoice at my violent death.

Bits of the story will be told. A piece to my wife, another piece to Rob. Some to my father, himself a veteran of an earlier, more deadly but somehow less appreciated war. Maybe in some inevitable combination of systematic, cathartic releases the entire story will be told, but never will just one person get it all. At least not spoken.

"Not now."

"OK. I love you." A silent prayer goes through my mind, thanking God for giving me this woman.

"I love you, too."

My kids take turns talking. My oldest comes on first, and I sit in a thankful receive mode as he relays his day to me. Summer being new, the freedom of no school hasn't lost its attraction yet. I smile involuntarily as he talks about riding his bike in enthusiastic detail and mentions the latest rumor about the Harry Potter movie we look forward to watching together. My daughter is next and she is young enough to still be enthralled with stuffed animals but old enough to tell me all the wonderful details in somewhat mature language. Something about Webkins. Again, it is nice just to listen to them talk.

My wife comes on again with my youngest, who's not quite two years old. She coaxes a few sounds out of him that hint toward "I love you, Daddy," but most certainly aren't. More than when I left nine months ago, however.

"I'll let you talk to Ben last. I love you. Have sweet dreams," she ends.

"I love you, too. I'll try," I answer and await the onslaught from my middle son, who is months shy of kindergarten.

"Hey, buddy," I begin. His talking must still be drawn out at first, but once started is essentially unstoppable.

"Hi, Daddy!" is the recognizable start, and then he unleashes an unintelligible torrent of enthusiastic verbiage. He has a speech problem that is exacerbated when he talks fast, which he does today. Toward the end, however, he quiets and asks slowly and solemnly, "Did you see any bad guy turtles today?" The age of cartoons has left him with a firmly developed sense of bad guys and good guys. Mentally, he has translated that into an animal that he sees as tough: the turtle. Every time I call he asks the same question, and I most always have to say, "Not today."

But not today.

"Yep!"

An audible gasp is heard on the other side of the world.

"Did you shoot them?"

"A few."

"So they aren't going to hurt those kids?" How does one explain to a child why I left for a year? If I miss a soccer game or a recital, I'd better have a good excuse. I am missing a whole year's worth of these, so I'd better have a *great* excuse. For my four-year-old, the only one I could think of was to show him pictures of the kids out here, who don't go to school and don't have a future. Then blame the bad guys for making their lives miserable. It is simplistic and arguably false, but it is all I had.

"Nope."

"Good." For a boy who talked for three straight minutes, he says more with that one word than the rest of the conversation combined. The ultimate arbitrator of today's events has spoken with the conviction and clarity that only a child can provide. A child like Ben is incapable of any deception that doesn't benefit himself. If you are fat, he will tell you. If you have done wrong, he will tell you. If I have done well, he will tell me, and he has. But with that brevity comes the recognition that the conversation is ending, so I have to close quickly before he just puts down the phone and walks away.

With this one-word blessing from Ben, I can turn off my alarm and crawl into my sleeping bag on my bunk without needing to question myself or my day as I lie there. I have been judged and found worthy. By my soldiers, my Afghan counterparts, my wife, and, most important of all, my son. I already know sleep will come easy tonight and look forward to it. I am ready for tomorrow, which I hope brings nothing but quiet. Write my reports, sip some tea with Sarjang, and find out who else we killed today. A nice dinner in the chow hall. Maybe a movie in the TOC with Rob and Han. It's time to disconnect from the fake world and rejoin the starlit Afghan reality.

"I gotta go, Ben. I love you."

"I love you, too, Daddy. Bye-bye."

"Bye-bye. Happy birthday, Ben."

A giggle is heard. "Thanks, Daddy." And the phone goes dead.